Waterloo
& Beyond
A Tourist Guide to the Battlefield, Museums & More

the Bradt Travel Guide

Antony Mason

edition
I

www.bradtguides.com

Bradt Travel Guides Ltd, UK

AUTHOR

Antony Mason has been writing about Belgium for some 20 years – a happy outcome of being married to a Belgian (a Walloon from Waterloo, as it happens). His *Cadogan Guide to Brussels, Bruges, Ghent & Antwerp* was first published in 1995. He is also the author of the *DK Top 10 Guide to Brussels, Bruges, Antwerp and Ghent* (first published 2004), and wrote most of the *DK Eyewitness Travel Guide to Belgium and Luxembourg* (first published 2009). He is the 'Brussels Expert' for the *Daily Telegraph* series of online city-break guides and writes occasional articles for the *Daily Telegraph* Saturday Travel section (eg: on the World War I centenary commemorations, and the wonders of Belgian *frites* (chips)). His first book for Bradt Travel Guides was *Mons: European Capital of Culture* (2014). His other recent Belgium-oriented publications include his translation and adaptation of *Le Goût des Belges* by Eric Boschman and Nathalie Derny, called *A Slice of Belgium* in the English edition (Racine, 2014), a humorous analysis of what the Belgians really eat.

Reprinted July 2015
First published March 2015
Bradt Travel Guides Ltd
IDC House, The Vale, Chalfont St Peter, Bucks SL9 9RZ, England
www.bradtguides.com
Print edition published in the USA by The Globe Pequot Press Inc,
PO Box 480, Guilford, Connecticut 06437-0480

ISBN: 978 1 78477 001 3 (print)
e-ISBN: 978 1 78477 110 2 (e-pub)
e-ISBN: 978 1 78477 210 9 (mobi)

British Library Cataloguing in Publication Data
A catalogue record for this book is available from the British Library

Photographs
Front cover Butte du Lion (©Jean-Philippe Van Damme)
Back cover Re-enactor ©Joseph Jeanmart/Whybelgium.co.uk; Hanging Gardens at Thuin ©WBT/JL Flémal
Title page Wellington, painted by Thomas Lawrence, 1828 (©Image Asset Management/SuperStock); Road sign (©Antony Mason); Butte du Lion (©WBT/JL Flémal)

Maps David McCutcheon FBCart.S

Typeset from the author's disc by Ian Spick
Production managed by Jellyfish Print Solutions; printed in Europe
Digital conversion by the www.dataworks.co.in

Contents

Belgian Tourist Office
Brussels • Wallonia

Le Brabant wallon

Prepared with the support of the Belgian Tourist Office and the Federation of Tourism for Walloon Brabant Province.

LIST OF MAPS

KEY TO MAP SYMBOLS

− − −	International border	✚	Pharmacy
═══	Motorway	🕯	Statue/monument
───	Main road	⊞	Historic/important building
───	Other road	🏺	Museum/gallery
⊶⊶⊶	Railway	😃	Theatre/cinema
✈	Airport	†	Church
坴	Theme park	🇫	Cemetery
🅿	Parking	❀	Garden
⛽	Petrol station	☀	Viewpoint
$	Bank	♧	Tree/wood
✉	Post office	🎋	Sports venue
ℹ	Tourist information	●	Other point of interest
		▦	Urban park

BATTLE MAPS

▰ Allied cavalry		◣ French cavalry		◣ Prussian cavalry	
▬ Allied infantry		▬ French infantry		▬ Prussian infantry	
♣ Allied artillery		♣ French artillery		♣ Prussian artillery	
➤ Allied advance/retreat		➤ French advance/retreat		➤ Prussian advance/retreat	

Introduction

The Battle of Waterloo took place 200 years ago. Europe is scarred with the sites of many battles, but few have the resonance of Waterloo. It was the culmination of the Napoleonic Wars, which – with the final defeat of the French Emperor – brought to a close two decades of turmoil in Europe. In this epic clash to the south of Brussels, the European Allies led by the Duke of Wellington and Marshal Blücher were pitched against the French led by Napoleon making a last-ditch attempt to regain control of his empire. The Allied victory, and the treaty settlements that followed, in many ways shaped modern Europe on the verge of universal industrialisation. But the outcome was in the balance until the final moments. 'A damned nice [delicate] thing, the nearest run thing you ever saw in your life,' declared Wellington afterwards.

The battlefield, to the south of the town of Waterloo, remains a landscape of rolling farmland – preserved under a law of 1914 – where it is still possible to trace and imagine every step of the conflict. But it is a blank canvas unless you have a guide to paint the scene, set it in context and explain the sights and monuments. This is the purpose of this book. There are many far more detailed studies of the Battle of Waterloo – it is one of the most written-about battles in history (see the list on page 73 for some of them). This is unashamedly a tourist guide, which tells readers about the battle and the battlefield, and also where to eat, drink and stay and how to make the most of their visit to Waterloo and its surroundings.

WHERE IS WATERLOO?

Waterloo is in Belgium, about 15km south of central Brussels. It is in the Province of Brabant Wallon (Walloon Brabant in English) in Wallonia, the French-speaking southern half of Belgium. Waterloo is the name of a small town (population 30,000), and the battlefield lies 4km to its south.

FEEDBACK REQUEST AND UPDATES WEBSITE

At Bradt Travel Guides we're aware that guidebooks start to go out of date on the day they're published – and that you, our readers, are out there in the field doing research of your own. You'll find out before us when a fine new family-run hotel opens or a favourite restaurant changes hands and goes downhill. So why not write and tell us about your experiences? Contact us on ☏01753 893444 or e info@bradtguides.com. We will forward emails to the author who may post updates on the Bradt website at www.bradtupdates.com/waterloo. Alternatively you can add a review of the book to www.bradtguides.com or Amazon.

PLEASE NOTE

At the time of publication, in early 2015, several of the key battlefield sites were still undergoing transformation in preparation for the bicentenary in June 2015. This applied in particular to the new Memorial of the Battle of Waterloo visitor centre due to be inaugurated in May 2015, the new museum on the battlefield at the Hameau du Lion, and the accompanying facilities. New developments were also under way at the Ferme de Hougoumont and the Ferme de Mont-Saint-Jean. The information given in this book is as up to date as it could be at that time. For confirmation of opening hours and admission prices, please consult the websites cited on page 6, or ask at the Tourist Information offices.

WATERLOO AND BEYOND WEBSITE

The Federation of Tourism for Walloon Brabant Province has created a useful and engaging English-language website entitled 'Visit Waterloo & Beyond' (www.waterlooandbeyond.be). It contains details of the Waterloo Bicentenary and the battlefield sites and attractions, as well as broader regional information, such as accommodation, what to see and do, sports facilities (eg golf) and local gastronomic specialities.

Practical Information

GETTING THERE AND AWAY

BY ROAD The town of Waterloo lies close to the motorway called the Ring, or R0, which encircles Brussels. Travellers coming from just about any direction, including the Channel ports from England, can head towards Brussels and take the Ring to reach Waterloo (exit 28 Waterloo Nord or exit 27 Waterloo Centre) and the battlefield (exit 26 Butte du Lion). The battlefield is linked to the centre of the town of Waterloo by the busy Brussels–Charleroi Road (the N5). This same road also leads north right to the heart of Brussels, on the Chaussée de Waterloo.

Although it is possible to visit most of the sights in this book by public transport and on foot, a car is useful because the sights are spread out over a wide area, and – although the battlefield is separated from Waterloo Town by just 4km – the road between them is not something you would want to walk along.

Cross-Channel ferry links from England The operators of these routes are in constant competition, so look around for the best deal to suit your needs. Dover–Calais: P&O Ferries (❍ 0871 664 6464; *www.poferries.com*); MyFerryLink (❍ 0844 248 2100; *www.myferrylink.com*). Dover–Dunkirk: DFDS Seaways (❍0871 574 7235; *www.dfdsseaways.co.uk*). P&O also operate an overnight service from Hull to Zeebrugge (the port of Bruges). Waterloo is 215km from Calais, and 137km from Zeebrugge.

Cross-Channel link from England by Eurotunnel This is the 'Shuttle' link between Folkestone and Coquelles (just west of Calais) (❍ 0844 335 3535; *www.eurotunnel.com*). Off-peak prices can be competitive with the ferries, and the 35-minute train ride on a car-transporter beneath the sea is a blessing in inclement weather.

BY TRAIN Waterloo is well connected by train: Brussels, a major rail hub, is just to the north. From the UK the easiest route is the London–Brussels Eurostar (❍ 0843 218 6186; *www.eurostar.com*). On arrival at the Brussels-Midi station, you simply have to change platforms to reach Waterloo. Trains in Belgium are operated by SNCB, which has an efficient English-language website (*www.belgianrail.be*).

For Waterloo Town (to visit the Musée Wellington, Chapelle Royale and Eglise Saint-Joseph, and the Tourist Office) there is the Waterloo station, 1km to the west of the centre, served by direct trains leaving Brussels-Midi station (and indeed Brussels-Central and Brussels-Nord) every hour. The journey from Brussels-Midi takes 24 minutes. You can take Bus W or 365a (see *By bus from Brussels*, page 3) from the centre of Waterloo to the battlefield.

For a station closer to the battlefield and the Butte du Lion (3km), there are two direct trains an hour to Braine-l'Alleud from Brussels-Midi (and also from Brussels-Central and Brussels-Nord). The journey from Brussels-Midi takes 16–28

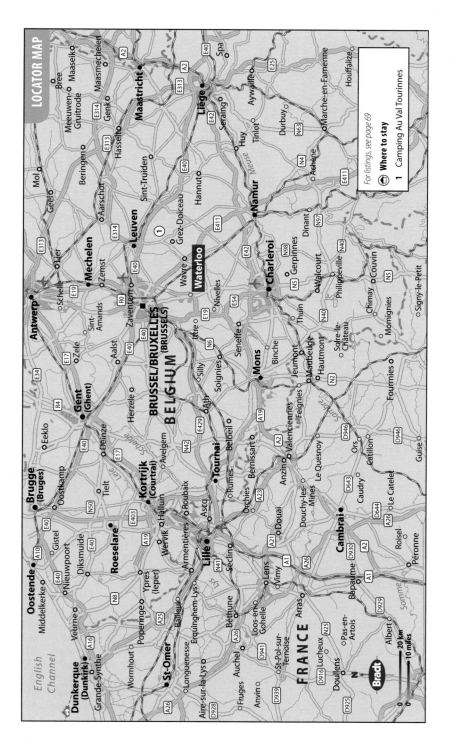

Cars can travel under the English Channel on Eurotunnel trains (© Eurotunnel)

minutes. You can take Bus W (see *By bus from Brussels*, below) from Braine-l'Alleud station to the Route de Nivelles (Esso) stop, which is 500m from the Butte du Lion.

BY AIR The nearest international airports are Brussels and Charleroi ('Brussels South'). Brussels is served by a number of operators in the UK. From London Heathrow: British Airways (*www.ba.com*) and Brussels Airlines (*www. brusselsairlines.com*). From London Gatwick: easyJet (*www.easyjet.com*). From Birmingham, Bristol and Edinburgh: Brussels Airlines (*www.brusselsairlines.com*). From Newcastle and East Midlands: bmi (*www.bmiregional.com*). There are regular rail links from the airport to Waterloo (*www.belgianrail.be*), changing at Brussels-Midi station (see page 1); the journey takes just over an hour.

From the UK, Charleroi Airport (40km south of Waterloo) is currently served by Ryanair (*www.ryanair.com*) out of Manchester only. From the airport you can go by bus to the railway station at Charleroi-Sud, then take the train to Braine-l'Alleud (the station closest to the battlefield); the journey takes 33 minutes. For Waterloo Town, change at Braine-l'Alleud for one stop; the journey from Charleroi-Sud takes about 50 minutes in total.

BY BUS FROM BRUSSELS Two buses from Brussels-Midi station, operated by TEC Brabant Wallon (*www.infotec.be*), serve both Waterloo Town (about 45 minutes) and the battlefield (about 1 hour). The Bus W (Brussels–Waterloo–Braine-l'Alleud) leaves Brussels-Midi railway station every hour or two hours throughout the day and travels to Waterloo town centre (get off at Eglise for the Eglise Saint-Joseph and Musée Wellington) then travels to the west of the battlefield (get off at the Route de Nivelles (Esso) stop for a short walk east (500m) to the Hameau du Lion) before heading to the railway station of Braine-l'Alleud.

Bus 365a (Brussels–Charleroi) also leaves from Brussels-Midi railway station every hour or two hours throughout the day and follows the same route to Waterloo town centre. But thereafter it continues on the N5 and stops at the battlefield at Wellington's crossroads and the Gordon Monument (get off at the stop called Monument Gordon), which is just 400m from the Hameau du Lion. It also stops at the Belle Alliance and the Musée du Caillou, and at Quatre-Bras, before heading on to Charleroi.

GETTING AROUND

ON FOOT Waterloo Town is an agreeable place to wander about, to shop and see the sights, but it has the busy N5 road running through it. The battlefield is essentially fields, crossed by tracks and paths, plus quiet roads around the Butte du Lion – again, agreeable to walk in and around (see pages 47–51 for a guided walk around the battlefield). The trouble is that there is no easy way, or at least agreeable way, to walk between the two. For walking around the battlefield sites, bring stout shoes: some of the paths are only farm tracks and get muddy after rain; some of the lanes are cobbled.

BY CAR The Waterloo area and battlefield are car-friendly, even if the main roads are almost always busy. Parking is usually easy enough. Note that for controlled public parking you will need a cardboard parking clock (available at the Tourist Office and at newsagents, and supplied with most hire cars) to show your arrival time; you are allowed two hours from arrival.

BY BUS See *By bus from Brussels*, page 3: the same services (Bus W and Bus 365a) are the ones that take visitors to and from Waterloo Town and Braine-l'Alleud and the battlefield.

BY TAXI There are taxi ranks at the railway stations at Waterloo and Braine-l'Alleud. Otherwise you have to ring for one and arrange a pickup – or get your restaurant or hotel to do it for you. Companies include Euro Taxis (*0473 69 72 20; www.eurotaxis.be*), Taxis Waterloo (*0475 253 903; www.taxiswaterloo.com*), and Taxis Fabbrimone (*02 354 28 41; www.taxisfabbrimone.com*).

BATTLE RE-ENACTMENTS

Every year, and especially every five years, hundreds of dedicated re-enactors from all over Europe come to Waterloo to recreate the battle on the weekend closest to 18 June. All volunteers, they are serious amateur historians, who take great pride in the historical accuracy of their uniforms, their weapons and the rest of the kit – which they have to acquire and pay for themselves. Most are affiliated to organisations such as the Napoleonic Association (*www.napoleonicassociation.org*). They attend training days beforehand, and practise firing their flintlock muskets with real gunpowder (but no musket balls), charging on horseback with swords drawn and firing artillery,

each according to his chosen station. They bivouac in all weathers in authentic style, cooking on open fires. Some act as surgeons. They are not only men: women recreate the roles of officers' wives, cooks, laundresses, seamstresses and general camp-followers (this is the subject of some controversy). They all live the role, in character. It is serious business – but fun, and deeply fulfilling to the participants who devote so much time and money to their hobby. The Battle of Waterloo is an especially popular re-enactment, taking place on or around 18 June, and the re-enactors turn out in big numbers. For the bicentenary in 2015: 5,000 re-enactors, 300 horses, 100 cannon – a small fraction of the original numbers, of course, but the world's biggest ever re-enactment.

A campaigner at a re-enactment (© Joseph Jeanmart/Whybelgium.co.uk)

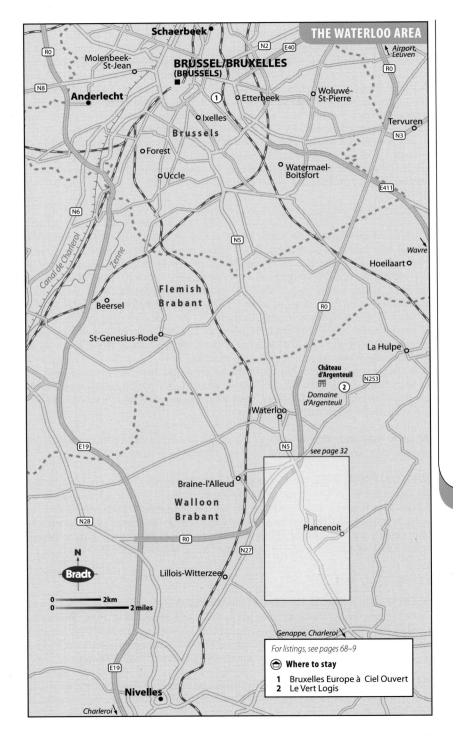

Schaerbeek

N2 E40

Airport,
Leuven

RO

Molenbeek-
St-Jean

BRUSSEL/BRUXELLES
(BRUSSELS)

RO

N8

Anderlecht

1 Etterbeek

Woluwé-
St-Pierre

Ixelles

Brussels

Tervuren

N3

Forest

Watermael-
Boitsfort

Uccle

E411

N6

Canal de Charleroi

Zenne

N5

Wavre

Hoeilaart

Flemish
Brabant

Beersel

RO

St-Genesius-Rode

La Hulpe

Château
d'Argenteuil

N253

2

Domaine
d'Argenteuil

Waterloo

E19

N5

see page 32

Braine-l'Alleud

Walloon
Brabant

N28

Plancenoit

RO

N

Bradt

N27

Lillois-Witterzee

0 ——— 2km
0 ——— 2 miles

Genappe, Charleroi

For listings, see pages 68–9

Where to stay

1 Bruxelles Europe à Ciel Ouvert
2 Le Vert Logis

E19

Nivelles

Charleroi

1

WHEN TO VISIT

Now is an excellent time: the 200th anniversary of the Battle of Waterloo has seen a major shake-up of the battlefield site. The battlefield centre, the Hameau du Lion, has been transformed by the new, innovative Memorial of the Battle of Waterloo visitor centre. The Ferme de Hougoumont and the Ferme de Mont-Saint-Jean have undergone major renovation, and the various museums have dusted themselves down and created new exhibitions and displays to mark the bicentenary.

The visitor centre and all the other major attractions are open all year. Most visitors will come spring–summer–autumn, taking advantage of more favourable weather to explore what is essentially an outdoor site. There is always a spike in midsummer around the anniversary of the battle on 18 June.

TOURS AND TOURIST INFORMATION

There is an excellent tourist office in the centre of Waterloo Town, opposite the Musée Wellington. For information when you can't visit in person, see their website (*www.visitwaterloo.be*). If you want to organise a private guided tour of the battlefield, see the website of the organisation called 'Guides 1815' (*www. guides1815.org*), which posts a list of tours currently available (in 11 languages), and a reservation form to fill in when you have made your choice. Guides 1815 is accredited by the Walloon Tourist Authority. As mentioned on page vi, the tourist office of the Province of Brabant Wallon (✆ *00 32 10 23 63 72*) also has a useful website covering the sights, attractions and tourist facilities of Waterloo and the province as a whole: *www.waterlooandbeyond.be*.

If you are planning a broader trip to Belgium, beyond Waterloo and its surroundings, the Belgian Tourist Office – Brussels and Wallonia (*217 Marsh Wall, London E14 9FJ;* ✆ *020 7531 0392; www.whybelgium.co.uk;* ✙ *@Whybelgium*) has plenty of information and ideas.

Maison du Tourisme de Waterloo *218 Chaussée de Bruxelles, 1410 Waterloo;* ✆ *02 352 09 10; www.visitwaterloo.be;* ☺ *Jun–Sep 09.30–18.00 daily, Oct–May 10.00–17.00 daily*

1815 WATERLOO PASS Look out for the 1815 Waterloo Pass, available at the Tourist Office as well as all the participating attractions. For a single fee (*currently adult/student/child 7–17 €13.50/€11/€8*) representing a 30% discount off the full price, you can visit all the major museums: the Musée Wellington, the Hameau du Lion (Memorial of the Battle of Waterloo visitor centre, Panorama) and the Ferme du Caillou (Napoleon's last HQ). Others may be added for 2015.

FESTIVALS AND EVENTS

WEEKEND AFTER SHROVE TUESDAY (FEBRUARY/MARCH) Carnival at Nivelles (*www. carnavaldenivelles.be*), the largest carnival in Walloon Brabant. It lasts from Saturday to Tuesday, but culminates in the parade (from 14.00) on Sunday, with 600 Gilles (dressed like the Gilles of Binche), plus Harlequins and Pierrots, giants and various floats. More parades follow on Monday (Carnaval Aclot) and Tuesday (Carnaval Raclot).

MAY–OCTOBER Marches de l'Entre-Sambre-et-Meuse: processions (or *marches*) in the region called Entre-Sambre-et-Meuse (to the south of Charleroi) in which holy relics or sacred images are carried along traditional routes accompanied by participants dressed in historic-style military uniforms, often Napoleonic, bearing rifles and accompanied by drums, pipes and bands. This military tradition is said to date back to the occupation of the region by the French (1794–1814), when many people had uniforms, which they stored after the defeat of Napoleon, and brought out later as fancy dress for special occasions. In 2012, UNESCO listed 15 of these *marches* as Masterpieces of the Oral and Intangible Heritage of Humanity. They include the *marches* of Thuin (third weekend in May), Walcourt (Trinity Sunday) and Ham-sur-Heure (the Sunday after 15 August).

Trinity Sunday (late May/June) The Tour Sainte-Renelde (*www.tourisme-roman-pais.be*) in Saintes, to the west of Waterloo, is a horseback procession involving 150–200 riders and mounted musicians, many dressed in various uniforms, some Napoleonic, leading relics of the patron saint in a 30km circuit around the parish. The tradition dates back to medieval times.

Weekend around 18 June Battle of Waterloo re-enactment (see page 4), with costumed battle reconstructions and bivouacs, weaponry displays, markets and guided tours.

First weekend of July Wavre 1815 (*www.wavre1815.com*): commemoration of the Battle of Wavre, with parades, markets and re-enactments.

Sundays in July/August Public carillon concerts at the Collegiate Church of St Gertrude, Nivelles, 16.00–17.00, best heard from the cloister (*www.tourisme-nivelles.be*).

Last Friday and Saturday in August The evocative, resonant and beautifully lit ruins of Abbaye de Villers are filled with song on the Nuit des Chœurs (Night of the Choirs; www.nuitdeschoeurs.be), with international choirs of all ages, sizes and singing styles, culminating in a musical firework display.

Weekend mid-September Annual Heritage Days (Journées du Patrimoine; *www.journeesdupatrimoine.be*). Access to various historic buildings not usually open to the public.

Last week in September Festival Mozart (*www.festival-mozart.be*), an international festival of chamber music, held in Waterloo at the Eglise Saint-Paul and the St John's Performing Arts Center (and also in Brussels and Genappe).

First Sunday after Michaelmas (29 September) Tour Sainte-Gertrude at Nivelles (*www.tourisme-nivelles.be*), when the reliquary of St Gertrude is taken on its horse-drawn carriage on a 15km tour through fields around

The Collegiate Church of St Gertrude, Nivelles (© Yves-Henri Feltz/MT Roman Païs)

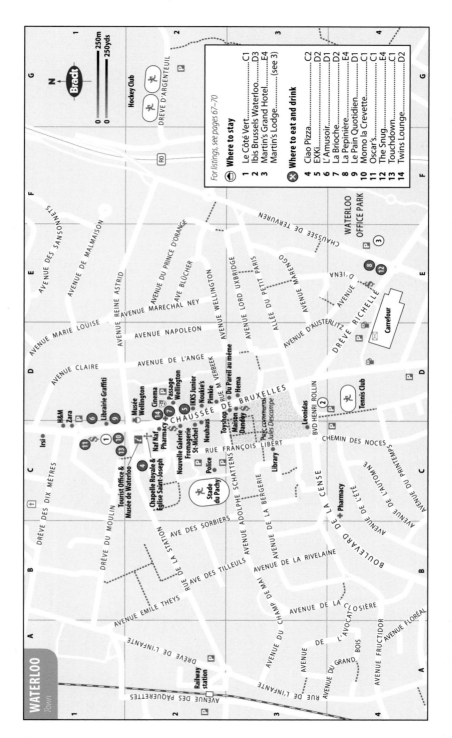

WATERLOO
Town

N Bradt

0   250m
0   250yds

For listings, see pages 67–70

ⓘ Where to stay

1	Le Côté Vert..............C1
2	Ibis Brussels Waterloo......D3
3	Martin's Grand Hotel......E4
	Martin's Lodge.......(see 3)

✕ Where to eat and drink

4	Ciao Pizza...............C2
5	EXKi.....................D2
6	L'Amusoir................D1
7	La Brioche...............D2
8	La Pepinière.............E4
9	Le Pain Quotidien.......D1
10	Momo la Crevette........C1
11	Oscar's.................C1
12	The Snug................E4
13	Touchdown..............C1
14	Twins Lounge...........D2

Hockey Club

DRÈVE D'ARGENTEUIL

AVENUE DES SANSONNETS

AVENUE DE MALMAISON

AVENUE MARIE LOUISE

AVENUE DU PRINCE D'ORANGE

AVENUE REINE ASTRID

AVENUE MARECHAL NEY

AVENUE BLÜCHER

AVENUE CLAIRE

AVENUE NAPOLEON

AVENUE DE L'ANGE

AVENUE WELLINGTON

AVENUE LORD UXBRIDGE

ALLÉE DU PETIT PARIS

AVENUE MARENGO

CHAUSSÉE DE TERVUREN

WATERLOO
OFFICE PARK

AVENUE D'AUSTERLITZ

DRÈVE RICHELLE

D'IENA

AVENUE

Carrefour

H&M
Zara
Librairie Graffiti

Irsi

Musée
Wellington
Cinema
Passage
Wellington
IKKS Junior
Noukie's
Pimkie
RUE M VERBEEK
Du Pareil au même
Hema
CHAUSSÉE DE BRUXELLES
Toyshop
Maison
Dandy
Leonidas

Tourist Office &
Musée de Waterloo

Naf Naf
Pharmacy
Nouvelle Galerie
Fromagerie
St-Michel
Neuhaus
Police

Chapelle Royale &
Église Saint-Joseph

Stade
du Pachy

BVD HENRI ROLLIN

Tennis Club

Parc communal
Jules Descampe

RUE FRANÇOIS LIBERT

Library

CHEMIN DES NOCES

DRÈVE DES DIX MÈTRES

DRÈVE DU MOULIN

RUE DE LA STATION

AVE DES SORBIERS

AVENUE EMILE THEYS

AVENUE ADOLPHE SCHATTENS

AVENUE DE LA BERGERIE

AVENUE DE LA RIVELAINE

BOULEVARD DE LA CENSE

AVENUE DE L'ÉTÉ

Pharmacy

AVENUE DE L'AUTOMNE

AVENUE DU PRINTEMPS

AVENUE DU CHAMP DE MAI

AVENUE DES TILLEULS

AVENUE DE LA CLOSIÈRE

AVENUE DE L'AVOCAT

AVENUE FLORÉAL

AVENUE FRUCTIDOR

AVENUE DU GRAND BOIS

AVENUE DE L'INFANTE

RUE DE L'INFANTE

AVENUE DES PAQUERETTES

Railway
station

DRÈVE DE L'INFANTE

8

the town, and then (in the afternoon) back into the centre, accompanied by a procession in medieval costume.

Third Sunday in October The Fête de Saint-Hubert, patron saint of hunters, is celebrated among the ruins of the Abbaye de Villers (*www.villers.be*) with a gathering and parade of mounted hunters, hunting horns and dogs of all kinds, and a sung mass and blessing of the animals in the abbey, plus food and drink and various other events.

FROM FIRST FRIDAY IN DECEMBER Marché de Noël (Christmas Market) at Nivelles (to the end of the following week; *www.tourisme-nivelles.be*) and Louvain-la-Neuve (to the end of the following fortnight; *www.louvainlaneige.be*).

PUBLIC HOLIDAYS IN BELGIUM
New Year's Day (Jour de l'An): 1 January
Easter Monday (Lundi de Pâques)
Labour Day (Fête du Travail): 1 May
Ascension Day (Jeudi de l'Ascension): sixth Thursday after Easter
Whit Monday (Lundi de Pentecôte): seventh Monday after Easter
National Day (Fête Nationale): 21 July
Assumption (Assomption): 15 August
All Saints' Day (Toussaint): 1 November
Armistice Day (Armistice de 1918): 11 November
Christmas Day (Noël): 25 December

SECURITY AND SAFETY

There should be little cause for concern in the Waterloo area, or indeed anywhere covered by this book – but of course all usual precautions should be observed.

SHOPPING

The main shopping area in the vicinity of the battlefield is in the town of Waterloo. Shops lie on a 1km-long strip on either side of the busy Chaussée de Bruxelles. That may not sound appealing, but the shops are of high quality, and there are two arcades where you can get away from the traffic. Along the way you will find numerous clothing boutiques, shoe and lingerie shops, plus polished pharmacies, opticians, banks and specialist outlets of all kinds.

There are several places to buy top-quality Belgian **chocolates**. Irsi has just two branches, one in Brussels (in Ixelles) and one here in Waterloo (*76 Chaussée de Bruxelles*), selling excellent handmade *pralines* (filled chocolates) and *pâtes de*

Local talent: Lio chocolates are made at Limal, near Wavre (© Lio)

Circus fun among the ruins of the Abbaye de Villers, a recommended excursion from Waterloo (© Joseph Jeanmart/Whybelgium.co.uk)

fruits (fruit jellies). Waterloo also has a branch of the top-ranking Neuhaus chain (*276 Chaussée de Bruxelles*), and a Leonidas (*2/12 Boulevard Henri Rolin*), which is widely respected for its high quality at affordable prices.

If you are looking for a gift that is not chocolate, try the exquisite **biscuits** of Maison Dandoy: this is famous for its wonderful shop close to the Grand'Place of Brussels, but it has a branch in Waterloo (*296 Chaussée de Bruxelles*).

For an excellent range of **cheeses**, including about 30 Belgian cheeses, go to the Fromagerie Saint-Michel (*244 Chaussée de Bruxelles*).

There are a number of **chain shops** in the Chaussée de Bruxelles, such as Zara and H&M (*at 113–115*), Pimkie (*211*), Naf Naf (*232*) and Hema (*249*), and the very cute **children's clothing** chain Du Pareil au même (*225*). There are more children's clothes at IKKS Junior (*171*) and Noukie's, for infants (*196*). The wonderful **toyshop** combining Le Zèbre à Pois and Fox & Compagnie under one roof (*294 Chaussée de Bruxelles*) specialises in wooden toys.

Of the two arcades, the Passage Wellington (*167 Chaussée de Bruxelles*) is the larger, and filled with shops selling clothes, shoes and jewellery. Note the Delvaux shop at the entrance, an outlet for the beautiful handcrafted leather handbags, made in Brussels since 1829, 'the oldest fine leather luxury house in the world'. Almost opposite is the Nouvelle Galerie (*238 Chaussée de Bruxelles*), with a similar range of shops.

The excellent **bookshop** Librairie Graffiti (*129–31 Chaussée de Bruxelles*) has a remarkable range of stock, primarily in French, but with a good selection of English books (novels, non-fiction, guidebooks, etc) upstairs.

For a big shop-up, or if you want to fill your car boot with Belgian beer and the more hardy (but excellent) brands of chocolate such as Galler (from Liège), there are two huge branches of the Carrefour **supermarket** chain, one on Drève Richelle (near the Ibis crossroads), and another even bigger – a Carrefour Planet Hypermarché – closer to the battlefield, by the roundabout just to the north of the Ferme de Mont-Saint-Jean. The car park of this Carrefour is the scene of Belgium's biggest weekly **open-air antiques and bric-a-brac market**, the Brocante Internationale de Waterloo (www.brocantedewaterloo.be), which takes place every Sunday morning until 14.00 (and also on public holidays).

WHAT TO SEE AND DO

A visit to Waterloo is essentially about the battlefield. It makes sense to do a bit of homework: the open fields and scattered farmhouses, peppered with plaques and monuments commemorating the battle, do not tell their own story. The museums can do that for you, but it's a steep learning curve if you arrive totally unprepared, and a much more rewarding experience if you can populate the battlefield with your imagination. The single most important site in the battlefield is the Hameau du Lion with the new Memorial of the Battle of Waterloo visitor centre. But the touchingly modest historic buildings set around the battlefield have the merit of being the places where real historical action took place. The Musée Wellington and the Ferme du Caillou were the headquarters of Wellington and Napoleon respectively, and both have small museums full of mementos and explanatory information. The Ferme de Hougoumont and the Ferme de Mont-Saint-Jean are soon to add to that list. Equipped with background knowledge, a walk around the battlefield really brings the battle alive, and shows what a critical role the terrain played in the outcome.

Waterloo is also a place to enjoy, with plenty of good places to stay and to eat and drink. Excursions within just 20km also provide a range of different pleasures – exceptional churches, the best museum dedicated to Tintin's creator Hergé and Belgium's top theme park, among others. For more ideas see the website www.waterlooandbeyond.be.

The battlefield today is still planted with cereal crops, as it was on 18 June 1815 – but then the rye grew to the height of a man and was wet with rain (© Joseph Jeanmart/Whybelgium.co.uk)

Practical Information   WHAT TO SEE AND DO

1

INFANTRY, CAVALRY, ARTILLERY

The armies of the Napoleonic Wars were made up of three complementary branches: infantry, cavalry and artillery. Each had its individual role, but each needed the support of the others to win battles. The infantry used muskets, which were notoriously inaccurate, and effective only to about 100m: to compensate for this, infantrymen needed to be massed in lines, two or three deep, to create a thick volume of fire. But lines were vulnerable to cavalry charges, so to advance in open ground the infantry formed columns 30 or so deep; here, though, only the outer ranks had the free space to fire their weapons. Columns were also very vulnerable to artillery: a cannonball could mow down an entire row of 30 men. So the infantry advanced in columns, then fanned out into lines to go into combat. If under attack from cavalry, they could quickly form 'squares', actually rectangles, four men deep on each side, with the two or three back rows firing muskets and the front row kneeling with fixed bayonets pointing outwards. Horses would not charge squares and cavalrymen could not reach into them to attack them. Infantry squares were almost unassailable by cavalry: however, like marching columns, they could suffer mass casualties from artillery. The artillery fired solid cannonballs (roundshot), or fused and exploding shells, or 'canister' (tins or leather pouches filled with about 85 iron balls, loosely referred to as 'grapeshot'), which was particularly deadly in close action against cavalry and infantry. Light cannons were drawn up by horse artillery especially to get close to the action. Artillery teams were vulnerable to enemy cannon fire, to cavalry charges and infantry attack.

The infantry on both sides used smoothbore, muzzle-loaded muskets. Their ammunition came in paper cartridges containing gunpowder and a lead musket ball about the size of a large marble. To load his musket, the infantryman bit off the end of the cartridge, put a small pinch of gunpowder into the priming pan next to the trigger, then tipped the rest of the gunpowder down the upended barrel, followed by the musket ball and the cartridge paper (to serve as the 'wad', to hold the ball in), all of which was then pushed home with the iron ramrod. When he pulled the trigger, the flint (literally a chip of stone flint) slammed forward and sparked the gunpowder, which ignited the gunpowder in the barrel to fire off the musket ball. A trained infantryman could fire a musket two or more times in a minute. If he did not have time to reload, he could fight hand-to-hand using the bayonet fixed to the tip of his musket. More accurate rifles (which had rifling in the barrel to spin the ball) were used by specialist rifle brigades; they could hit a target at 200m, although rifles took longer to load. Armed with rifles or muskets, trained 'light infantry' marksmen called skirmishers (*voltigeurs* or *tirailleurs* in French) went ahead of the lines and attacking columns to fight independently, picking off officers, non-commissioned officers and the drummers signalling their commands.

The line, two or three deep, was the main formation for infantry engagement (©Joseph Jeanmart/ Whybelgium.co.uk)

2

History

HISTORICAL TIMELINE

1789 The French Revolution begins with the storming of the Bastille

1792 The French Revolutionary Army invades the Austrian Netherlands (Belgium) and wins a victory at Jemappes

1794 The French Revolutionary Army scores another victory at Fleurus and occupies Belgium

1799 Napoleon seizes power in France in a coup

1804 Napoleon crowns himself Emperor of the French

1807 The Peninsular War begins in French-occupied Portugal; Arthur Wellesley leads the British army (from 1808)

1812 The French army invades Russia and is forced to retreat with massive losses; the British under Wellesley win a great victory over the French in Spain at Salamanca

1813 Wellesley scores another victory in Spain at Vitoria; Napoleon is defeated decisively at the Battle of Leipzig

1814 Napoleon abdicates (April) and is sent to rule Elba; Arthur Wellesley formally becomes 1st Duke of Wellington (May); the Congress of Vienna convenes to decide how to provide long-term peace in Europe (September)

1815 **28 February** Napoleon lands in southern France after escaping from Elba

13 March The Allies declare Napoleon an outlaw

15 March Under the Congress of Vienna, the Kingdom of the Netherlands is created, embracing Belgium

19 March The French King Louis XVIII flees to Ghent

20 March Napoleon resumes power in Paris; his 'Hundred Days' begins

25 March The Allies declare war on Napoleon; mobilisation begins

15 June Napoleon's Armée du Nord crosses the border into Belgium; the Duchess of Richmond holds her ball in Brussels

16 June Napoleon defeats the Prussians under Blücher at Ligny; the French under Marshal Ney fight an indecisive battle against the Anglo-Allied forces at Quatre-Bras

17 June In heavy rain, Wellington retreats to Mont-Saint-Jean (Waterloo); Blücher retreats to Wavre; Napoleon sets up his HQ at the Ferme du Caillou

18 June The Battle of Waterloo

11.30 The battle begins with a French attack on the Ferme-Château de Hougoumont

13.30 The French under Lieutenant General d'Erlon launch their first main attack on Wellington's left and are repulsed by heavy cavalry

16.00 Marshal Ney orders the French cavalry to attack the Anglo-Allied right; the attack fails

18.00 Plancenoit, on Napoleon's right, is taken by the Prussians, then retaken by the French Young Guard

18.30 Marshal Ney attacks the Anglo-Allied right and centre and takes the Ferme de la Haie Sainte

19.30 Napoleon sends the Imperial Guard to attack Wellington's right

20.00 The French are forced by the Prussians to retreat from Plancenoit, as Ziethen's Prussian I Corps links up with Wellington's left

20.30 The Imperial Guard is repulsed; the French retreat; Wellington orders a general advance, turning the retreat into a rout; Napoleon flees the battlefield

22.00 Wellington meets Blücher at La Belle Alliance and they congratulate each other as victors

21 June Wellington's Victory Dispatch reaches London

22 June Napoleon abdicates in Paris for a second time

3 July The Allied army occupies Paris

8 July Louis XVIII is restored to the throne of France

15 July Napoleon surrenders to the British near Rochefort, southwest France

7 August Napoleon is put on board HMS *Northumberland*, bound for St Helena

1817 The Gordon Monument is erected at Waterloo, the first battlefield monument

1818 The Hanoverian Monument is erected

1819 The Prussian Monument is erected at Plancenoit

1821 Napoleon dies on St Helena

1826 The Butte du Lion is inaugurated

1830 Belgium wins its independence from the Netherlands

1904 This Wounded Eagle Monument is inaugurated

1912 The Waterloo Panorama is opened

Chasseurs of the French Imperial Guard at a re-enactment (© M Fasol)

1914 The Monument to the Belgians is inaugurated; the Waterloo battlefield is protected by law

2015 The bicentenary is marked by the opening of the Memorial of the Battle of Waterloo visitor centre, the new scenography at Ferme du Caillou and Ferme de Hougoumont

BEFORE 1815

On 18 June 1815 Belgium did not even exist as a nation, but many of its inhabitants – who lined up on both sides of the battlefield – hoped that, at long last, it soon would. Belgium had been fought over, overrun and occupied by foreign rulers since ancient times. After Julius Caesar had defeated the Belgae ('the bravest of the Gauls') in 57BC, their lands became Roman, then Frankish. Belgium's convenient location in the centre of northern Europe made it a vibrant trading hub: Bruges, Brussels, Ghent, Antwerp and Ypres prospered in medieval times. But by the same token it was a strategic prize, contested by the Kings of France, the Germanic Dukes of Lorraine and the Prince-Bishops of Liège, allied to the Holy Roman Emperor. After a golden age of rule by the duke of Burgundy in the 15th century, most of Belgium became part of the Spanish Netherlands (1579–1713), then the Austrian Netherlands (1713–94), until the French Revolutionary Armies swept through and absorbed it into France, frustrating a nascent Belgian independence movement. With good reason, since the 17th century, Belgium has been nicknamed 'the cockpit of Europe'.

HISTORY OF THE BATTLE OF WATERLOO

In 1815 Waterloo was just a little rustic hamlet on the main road into Brussels from Charleroi and the border with France, at the point where the road entered the great Soignes forest. It had a coaching inn, and cottages where foresters and farmworkers lived, and – its main landmark – an unusually elaborate, but dilapidated, Baroque Chapelle Royale, built on a whim by a governor of the Spanish Netherlands in 1690. Despite this unremarkable backdrop, when – on the morning of 18 June – the sun rose over rain-sodden fields and farms a few miles to the south of Waterloo, to many of the 123,000 soldiers gathered there it seemed that a day of destiny of European, even global, dimensions had dawned.

In April 1814 Napoleon had abdicated, forced at last to abandon his formerly glorious role as Emperor of the French and master of continental Europe. It had been a tumultuous 20 years. Out of the bloody chaos of the French Revolution of 1789, Republican France had turned into an aggressive military power to fend off the monarchies that surrounded it. The Austrian Netherlands – of which Belgium was then part – was an early target, and France won a victory at Jemappes in 1792, and again in 1794 at Fleurus, to take control. A charismatic young officer called Napoleon Bonaparte led the French Revolutionary army into Italy before seizing power in France in 1799. Turning his back on the Revolution, he soon adopted the trappings of the old monarchies and aristocracy, crowning himself Emperor in 1804. Then, through military aggression and diplomacy, he extended his empire across Europe – the German states, Austria, Poland, Spain and Portugal. Despite the massive toll in blood and money that this adventure took, he remained unassailably popular, in France and in many of the conquered states, where a new order promised fulfilment to many talented people previously stifled by the closed shop of monarchy.

Napoleon Buonaparte, later restyled Bonaparte (1769–1821), was 45 at the Battle of Waterloo. A young and charismatic officer of modest origins from Corsica (newly a part of France), he had risen rapidly through the ranks of the Republican army in post-Revolutionary France and seized power in a coup in 1799. As self-appointed Emperor of the French, from 1804 to 1814, he had been the ruler of most of Europe, won by his brilliance as a military commander and held by the popularity of his liberal and egalitarian reforms in the monarchies that he overthrew. He brought changes to the structure of society, to government administration, to the law with the Code Napoléon, to education and religion; he promoted trade and industry, and talent. In France, and among many of his imperial subjects, he was the focus of cultist adoration, which forgave him for taking on the grandiose trappings and personal enrichment of the old aristocracy. On the battlefield he was the mastermind who gave the overall orders, but he delegated responsibility for enacting them to his commanders. At Waterloo, however, he was surrounded by commanders of less certain talents. He himself was overweight, uncharacteristically lethargic and possibly unwell. France was not going to forgive him for failure a second time.

Napoleon's bicorne hat, worn crossways, was an integral part of his public image
(© WBT/Alex Kouprianoff)

ELBA By 1809, of the major powers, only Britain stood against him. Napoleon tried to squeeze Britain into submission through a trade embargo called the Continental System, and in 1812, to enforce compliance, he invaded Russia. It was a catastrophe: of the 400,000 French and Allied troops who began that campaign, just 40,000 returned. Meanwhile the British, led by General Arthur Wellesley (later, from 1814, the 1st Duke of Wellington), had been making steady progress through Portugal and Spain in the Peninsular War, winning decisive victories at Salamanca (1812) and Vitoria (1813). Wellington crossed the Pyrenees into France in 1813, as Allies in the east rose to push the French back into France. Napoleon still rallied, winning a series of victories culminating in the Battle of Dresden in August 1813, but after defeat at the Battle of Leipzig in October, and the surrender of Paris in March 1814, the game was up. His commanders persuaded him to abdicate and surrender.

But what should become of him? Any punishment might have been suitable, given the years of suffering he had inflicted upon Europe. But the victorious Allies were sensitive to Napoleon's enduring popularity and anxious not to make a martyr of him. They decided instead to send him to rule over the little island of Elba, off the coast of Italy, a speck of his former empire, where he could live in some style with an allowance, but under strict orders not to leave, enforced by the British navy. The Allies meanwhile met at the Congress of Vienna to redraw the map of monarchist Europe, and find a path to enduring peace. France was ruled by the obese King Louis XVIII, grandson of Louis XV, at the head of an incompetent regime of returning aristocrats and turncoat Napoleonic generals. Belgium, in 1815, became part of the new Kingdom of the Netherlands under William I.

It did not take long for Napoleon to feel that he was needed back in his old country. He was bored and frustrated on Elba; his allowance failed to materialise; he heard rumours that the Allies might ship him further afield to some remote island in the South Atlantic. So, on 26 February 1815, he boarded a ship with 1,028 men and escaped Elba, landing on the south coast of France at Golfe-Juan two days later. He then began his march on Paris. It was an absurdly high-risk strategy, but typical of his captivating panache. In Paris Marshal Michel Ney, one of Napoleon's former generals, was dispatched by Louis XVIII to arrest him, and set off promising famously to 'bring him back in an iron cage'. Napoleon meanwhile was cheered all along the way, as old soldiers dropped everything to join his swelling ranks, raising the familiar cheer '*Vive l'Empereur!*' On 7 March, when vastly superior French forces confronted him south of Grenoble, Napoleon walked out alone and unarmed to meet them, at which point the entire army mutinied. Ney himself switched sides on 18 March. As more troops and generals joined him, Louis XVIII saw the writing on the wall and fled to Belgium. By 20 March Napoleon was back in Paris, and once again the ruler of France. His extraordinary 'Hundred Days' back in power had begun.

OUTNUMBERED The Allies gathered at the Congress of Vienna were stunned by this turn of events. Despite Napoleon's vows of peace, they knew he was a warmonger, and so declared war, not on France but on Napoleon himself, an outlaw. They quickly began to assemble their armies to invade. They could muster 850,000 men to attack France from all sides: Spain, Italy, Austria, the German states, Russia and Britain. Napoleon had just 250,000 men. But Napoleon knew that it would take the Russians (200,000 men) and the Austrians (210,000 men) weeks to reach his borders. If he could strike the Allies quickly and decisively, he stood a chance of splitting them and breaking the Alliance.

The immediate threat came from the Kingdom of the Netherlands (Belgium), where Wellington – whom he had never actually confronted in battle – had been put in charge of a mixed force of British, Dutch and Belgian troops, plus soldiers from various German states: Nassau, Brunswick and Hanover. They numbered 120,000, but this Anglo-Allied force was a mixed bag of experienced soldiers and raw, untried recruits: many of Wellington's best and most trusted soldiers, veterans of the Peninsular War, were in America fighting the War of 1812 (1812–15). But he was soon to be joined by the Prussians under the indomitable Field Marshal Gebhard Leberecht von Blücher, aged 72, at the head of another 130,000 men.

Back in France, Napoleon had to spread his 250,000 men around the country to fend off attack from all quarters. But he decided to concentrate a force of 123,000 men in the northeast, the Armée du Nord. They were, for the most part, loyal, experienced volunteers, including the feared 20,000-strong Imperial Guard (the Young Guard, Middle Guard and Old Guard), elite troops who prided

themselves on being undefeated. If Napoleon could cross the border into the Kingdom of the Netherlands swiftly and head for Brussels, he could drive a wedge between the Anglo-Allied forces and the Prussians. Then, with his 123,000 men, he could face opposing forces of 120,000 and 130,000 men one at a time. The key was not to allow Wellington and Blücher to join forces.

THE DUCHESS OF RICHMOND'S BALL In June 1815, Brussels was a flurry of activity. The various Anglo-Allied armies and the Prussians were encamped in a broad sweep of countryside to the south and southwest, and the city itself was full of officers, many accompanied by their wives. On the night of 15 June the Duchess of Richmond held a grand ball in the centre of Brussels, in a converted coach-house, attended by most of the leading officers, including Wellington. The city, however, was on edge: there were rumours that Napoleon had crossed the border and was heading for Brussels either through Mons or through Charleroi. Wellington refused to react until he knew which. The Duchess had offered to cancel the ball, but Wellington insisted it take place: he wanted to exhibit placid calm. Also, the ball meant that his officers would be gathered under one roof.

This proved fortuitous. During the ball, news confirmed that Napoleon's Armée du Nord had indeed broken across the border and was heading rapidly towards Charleroi, knocking Prussian resistance out of its path. 'Napoleon has humbugged me,' Wellington said. 'He has gained twenty-four hours' march on me.' To block Napoleon's route to Brussels, Dutch–Belgian infantry led by the young Prince of Orange (son of King William I) and Prince Bernhard of Saxe-Weimar, plus contingents of Brunswickers and Nassauers, had taken up positions at a strategic crossroads called Quatre-Bras: it lay at the place where the Brussels–Charleroi road intersected with the Nivelles–Namur road, 15km north of Charleroi, 30km south of Brussels (and 15km south of Waterloo). Meanwhile, the Prussians had concentrated their troops at a village called Ligny, 10km southeast of Quatre-Bras, which stood at strategically important river crossings to the south of the Namur road. Roads were the issue at stake: they were the vital arteries along which armies could move artillery and supplies. The entire road between Charleroi and Brussels had been paved with cobbles by the Austrians, for this very purpose.

LIGNY AND QUATRE-BRAS Wellington set off from Brussels early on Friday 16 June to meet Blücher at a windmill at Brye (also known as Bussy) near Ligny. He assured Blücher that he would send troops to support him at Ligny, if he could. He also advised Blücher to place his troops on the reverse side of the ridge on which they were lined up, to shelter them from artillery fire (it was one of Wellington's characteristic tactics and a secret of many of his successes) but Blücher's tetchy chief of staff Field Marshal August Gneisenau dismissed this out of hand, saying that Prussians like to see their enemy. This obstinacy proved fatal. Battle commenced at Ligny at 14.30, with 82,700

Field Marshal Arthur Wellesley, the 1st Duke of Wellington (1769–1852), was 46 at the Battle of Waterloo. Born in Dublin into a wealthy aristocratic Anglo-Irish family, he had cut his military teeth in India, and was the hero of a triumphant campaign against the French in the Peninsular War (1807–14). Cool and aloof, he was not exactly loved by his men, but he commanded great respect and loyalty. Preparation was everything. He saw that his men were well provisioned, and was strict about never stealing food from locals. Dressed immaculately but unflamboyantly like a civilian in a dark blue jacket, cloak and white trousers and with a cocked hat, he was immediately recognisable to his troops. At Waterloo, he was always calm, as he went up and down the lines on his horse Copenhagen, issuing orders. In contrast to Napoleon, he took a hands-on approach to battlefield leadership, at the risk of exposing himself to danger. Many of his close colleagues lost their lives or were badly wounded – a fate that might easily have befallen him. Rewarded and honoured by the nation, he had a long and distinguished career after Waterloo. His terms as Prime Minister (1828–30 and 1834) damaged his popularity – he is known as the 'Iron Duke' because of the iron shutters he put up on Apsley House, his residence in London, against rioters in 1831–32 – but nothing eclipsed his reputation as the victor of Waterloo.

Prussians facing 60,800 French, directed by Napoleon himself. The French artillery, famed for their power and efficiency, rapidly mauled the Prussians, who were forced to retreat. Blücher himself suffered a fall and was trapped for a while under his horse, but doggedly remounted. Ligny was Napoleon's last victory.

Meanwhile, at Quatre-Bras, 20,000 French troops under Marshal Ney faced 8,000 Dutch infantry and the German contingents. This was a winnable confrontation for the French: the Dutch and Germans were pushed back. But Ney, perhaps fearing that Wellington was holding superior forces in reserve, as was his wont, failed to press home his advantage. Gradually the Dutch were reinforced by British and Allied troops, and after Wellington arrived to take over command he had some 24,000 men in the field and was able to repulse the French and secure the crossroads. But it was now too late to send help to the Prussians – which to some Prussians looked like treachery.

All the while 17,000 French infantry and 1,700 cavalry, under Lieutenant General Jean-Baptiste Drouet, Count d'Erlon, following a series of conflicting orders, spent the afternoon dashing back and forth between Ligny and Quatre-Bras, where his forces could have made a decisive difference, but intervening in neither.

With the Prussians in retreat after their defeat at Ligny, Wellington could no longer hold his position at Quatre-Bras, so on 17 June he ordered a withdrawal. Retreat is a time of fatal vulnerability for armies. At Ligny and at Quatre-Bras the French could have driven home their advantage, but both Napoleon and Ney failed to take this opportunity. Furthermore, Blücher did not retreat east along his line of supply as Napoleon might have expected, but courageously went north to Wavre, where he could remain in contact with Wellington's forces.

Wellington was thus able to conduct an orderly retreat north, along the Brussels road. The weather had now turned foul: it poured with rain throughout 17 June, which drenched his troops but also discouraged pursuit. He stopped his forces at a ridge called Mont-Saint-Jean. The previous year, when reviewing the defences of the Kingdom of the Netherlands, Wellington had seen this ridge and shallow valley

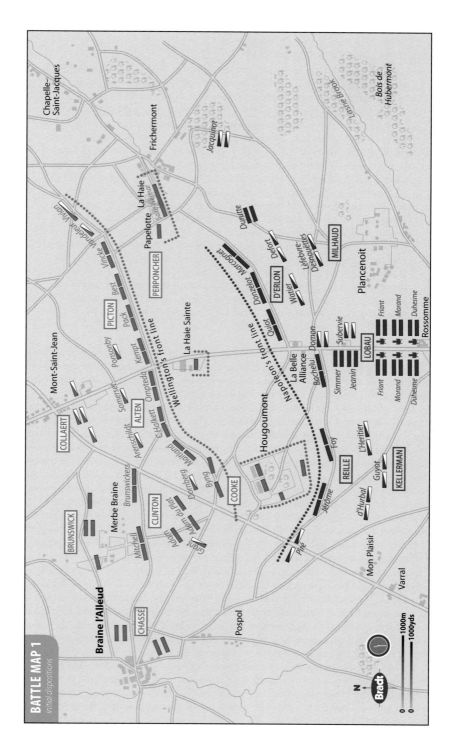

Chapelle–Saint-Jacques

Frichermont

Bois de Hubermont

La Haie
Papelotte

Jacquinot

Durutte

Marcognet

Défort

Lefebvre-Desnouëttes

MILHAUD

Vandeleur Vivian

Vincke

Best

Donzelot

D'ERLON

Watier

PERPONCHER

PICTON

Pack

Plancenoit

Ponsonby

Kempt

Quiot

La Haie Sainte

Wellington's front line

Subervie

Friant

Morand

Duhesme

Mont-Saint-Jean

Ompteda

Somerset

Domon

LOBAU

Rossomme

Napoleon's front line

Bachelu

Friant

Morand

Duhesme

Arenschildt

ALTEN

C Halkett

La Belle Alliance

Simmer

Jeanin

COLLAERT

Maitland

Hougoumont

Foy

L'Héritier

Byng

Dornberg

REILLE

Guyot

KELLERMAN

Brunswickers

CLINTON

COOKE

Jérôme

d'Hurbal

BRUNSWICK

Adam du Plat

Grant

Mitchell

Pire

Mon Plaisir

Merbe Braine

Adam

Varral

Braine l'Alleud

CHASSÉ

Pospol

N

Bradt

0 ——— 1000m
0 ——— 1000yds

20

as the perfect place to defend Brussels from attack from the south. He now left his men to bivouac in the rain along the ridge, or in and around three large farmhouses that punctuated his defensive line, and which were to serve as makeshift fortresses: the Ferme-Château de Hougoumont in the west, the Ferme de la Haie Sainte in the middle, and the Ferme de la Papelotte (and smaller Ferme de la Haie) in the east, spanning a distance of 3.5km in all. Then he retired to his headquarters in a coaching inn 4km to the north, in the little village of Waterloo.

DELAYED START Napoleon had reassembled the bulk of his army to follow Wellington. On 17 June, he made his headquarters at the Ferme du Caillou, 4km south of Wellington's ridge. He sent Marshal Emmanuel de Grouchy with 33,000 men to pursue the Prussians at Wavre, and – above all – to prevent them from joining Wellington.

On the morning of Sunday 18 June, Napoleon came forward from his battlefield headquarters at Rossomme to the inn called La Belle Alliance to review his troops as they marched onto the battlefield, bands playing, drums beating, and with repeated chants of '*Vive l'Empereur!*' They lined the southern ridge overlooking the shallow valley of Mont-Saint-Jean, on either side of La Belle Alliance. The artillery was positioned all along the front of the ridge, with infantry behind, and cavalry behind them. The Imperial Guard was kept in reserve, ready to deliver the *coup de grâce* at the end of the battle, as they had done in so many of Napoleon's victories. Wellington's forces were similarly arrayed along the opposite ridge – except that many of them were out of sight, hidden on the reverse slope of the ridge. That was unsettling for the French: they did not know quite what they were facing.

Separated by a distance of about 1km, the French side, numbering 48,000 infantry, 14,000 cavalry and 246 cannons, faced the Anglo-Allied forces of 50,000 infantry, 11,000 cavalry and 156 cannons. Among the Anglo-Allied forces were 17,000 Dutch and Belgian troops, and, from the German states, 11,000 from Hanover, 6,000 from Brunswick and 3,000 from Nassau. In other words, nearly two-thirds of Wellington's army was non-British.

Wellington was playing a defensive game: it was for the French to take the initiative and attack. The odds were slightly in favour of the French, but Wellington knew he could stand here because, earlier that morning, Blücher had promised that the Prussians would come to his aid, even though Wellington had failed to deliver his at Ligny. Wellington took up position at an elm tree on a crossroads on the Brussels–Charleroi road, his command post at the centre of his lines, to which he would frequently return.

The weather had cleared, but the ground was still sodden – so sodden that the mud would suck men's boots off, horses would be slowed to a laborious walk, and – most significant of all – low-flying cannonballs would sink and stop where they landed rather than bounce and scud through lines of infantry and cavalry, taking scores of victims. In addition, the fields were full of wet crops, including rye which, in those days, would grow nearly 2m tall.

Napoleon decided to wait until the ground dried. The morning drifted on to the nervous sound of drums, bands, bugles, shouted orders. They waited. Finally, with a burst of French cannon fire at about 11.30, the last battle of the Napoleonic Wars began – and one of the most brutal, a battle in which the aim of both sides was annihilation.

FIRST BLOOD Napoleon's opening gambit was to attack the Ferme-Château de Hougoumont on the far right of the Anglo-Allied lines, hoping to make Wellington reinforce it from the centre. He put his brother Prince Jérôme Bonaparte – not

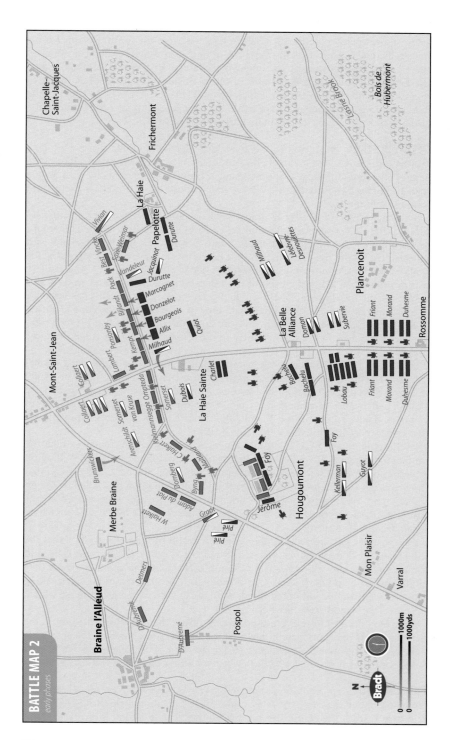

Chapelle–Saint-Jacques

Frichermont

Bois de Hubermont

La Haie

Lasne Brook

Vivian

Vincke

Best

Pack

Papelotte

Jacquinot

Vandeleur

Durutte

Vieux-Weimar

Durutte

Marcognet

Bijlandt

Donzelot

Ponsonby

Bourgeois

Lambert

Allix

Kempt

Milhaud

Milhaud

Lefebvre-Desnouëttes

Quiot

Plancenoit

Mont-Saint-Jean

Collaert

Collaert

Subervie

Domon

Friant

Morand

Duhesme

Somerset

von Kruse

Arenschildt

Ompteda

Kielmannsegge

Dubois

Charlet

La Belle Alliance

Rossomme

Friant

Morand

Duhesme

La Haie Sainte

Bachelu

Bachelu

Lobau

Somerset

Chassé

Friant

Morand

Duhesme

Brunswickers

Mauduit

Foy

Byng

Adam du Plat

Vincke

Domberg

Foy

Kellerman

Guyot

W Halkett

Merbe Braine

Graaf

Jérôme

Hougoumont

Piré

Piré

Mon Plaisir

Varral

Detmers

Pospol

Braine l'Alleud

D'Aubremé

D'Aubremé

N

Bradt

0 ___ 1000m

0 ___ 1000yds

Hougoumont after the battle, with the ruined château on the left (© Morphart Creation/Shutterstock.com)

famed for his competence – in charge of this task. The French had to storm the farm through a tangle of woods and across open ground. Despite being massively outnumbered, Scots and Coldstream guards, Nassauers and Hanoverians held onto Hougoumont throughout the day, tying down thousands of French troops.

Meanwhile, the French artillery pounded the Anglo-Allied lines with cannon fire. The ridge protected the troops to some degree: they were ordered to retreat and lie down. Nonetheless, the losses were alarming. At 13.30, the French launched their first main attack, when 17,000 infantry under the leadership of Lieutenant General D'Erlon, marched in columns across the fields to attack Wellington's left, defended by lines of Anglo-Allied infantry, mainly British and Hanoverians. The deep French columns marched forward at the *pas de charge*, to the beat of drums: 'the rum dum, the rum dum, the rummadum dummadum, dum, dum,' as one British officer described it, interspersed with shouts of '*Vive l'Empereur!*' – a terrifying sound to the young recruits in Anglo-Allied lines. There were many deserters.

Meanwhile, French troops led by Lieutenant General Pierre Durutte had taken the Ferme de la Haie on Wellington's far left, and was putting pressure on the Ferme de la Papelotte, defended by a Nassau regiment. As D'Erlon's columns advanced, their left flank was raked by fire from the contingent of the King's German Legion (a trusted unit of the British army made up of expatriate Germans) holding the Ferme de la Haie Sainte, and by British riflemen hiding in the sandpit-quarry beside it. The French broke out into a thin attack line and a fierce struggle took place along the road at the top of the ridge. The French seemed to be gaining the upper hand when the Anglo-Allied infantry counterattacked with a bayonet charge through the hedges that lined the road. During this attack Lieutenant General Sir Thomas Picton, commander of Wellington's left flank, was killed by a musket ball to the head – the highest-ranking officer among the Allies to fall at Waterloo. Then two brigades of British heavy cavalry, with some 2,600 horses, under the command of Lord Uxbridge, launched their attack – a nightmare for infantry still in lines and unable to form defensive squares. The Scots Grey Dragoons in particular wrought havoc among the French, who were forced into a chaotic retreat. The French lost two eagles, their precious regimental standards – a terrible humiliation. But the cavalry – always something of a law unto themselves – then failed to heed the recall and charged on into the valley to take on the French artillery. They were lacerated by enemy fire and forced to retreat; with their horses now exhausted and mired in the mud, they were picked off by the lighter lancers of the French cavalry. About half of the British cavalry in this charge was lost.

NEY'S MISTAKE The valley now emptied of all but the dead and the wounded, screaming and groaning in pain, men and horses. Stragglers from both sides robbed the fallen enemy of their valuables: a perk of soldiery. Then the French artillery began a second major cannonade. At about 16.00, Marshal Ney, sensing an Anglo-Allied retreat (in fact the evacuation of casualties and prisoners), gathered 4,800 cavalry and began a charge against the Anglo-Allied right flank. This was unusual: battles could not be won by cavalry charges alone. The cavalry's task was to pick off infantry in lines and gunners around their cannons; they could not defeat infantry once they had formed squares, hedged by bayonets and spitting musket balls. Several French generals pointed this out, but Ney – known as the 'the bravest of the brave' – was adamant. So in they went, led by the Cuirassiers in their glittering breastplates. First they were torn apart by British cannon firing roundshot and canister (grapeshot), then they charged helplessly around the 27 squares under a hail of musket fire. After their initial failure they were joined by some 4,200 heavy cavalry. Together they made perhaps seven charges. In between charges the French horse artillery rained roundshot and shells down on the squares, to more devastating effect. Finally, after about two hours, the French cavalry retreated, leaving their many dead and wounded behind them. Not one of the squares had broken. The attack had failed.

Napoleon was now under pressure. The Prussians were coming from the east. What, he wondered, had happened to Grouchy? He desperately needed Grouchy's 33,000 men at Waterloo. The answer was that Grouchy was entangled in another

Wellington trusted the resilience of his loyal British redcoats, such as the Black Watch and the Coldstream Guards (© Joseph Jeanmart/Whybelgium.co.uk)

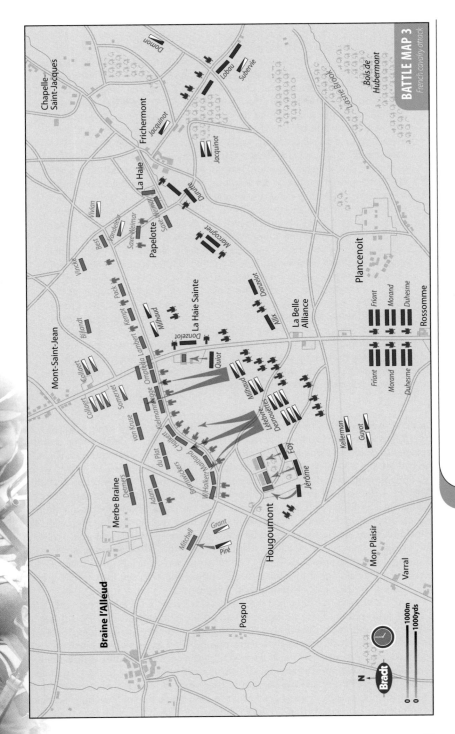

BATTLE MAP 3
French cavalry attack

Chapelle–Saint-Jacques

Bois de Hubermont

Lasne Brook

Frichemont

Jacquinot

Lobau

Subervie

Domon

Jacquinot

La Haie

Durutte

Plancenoit

Vivian

Vandeleur

Best

Saxe-Weimar

Saxe-Weimar

Papelotte

Marcognet

Friant

Morand

Duhesme

Vincke

Durutte

Donzelot

Rossomme

Pack

Kempt

Milhaud

Allix

Friant

Morand

Duhesme

Mont-Saint-Jean

Bijlandt

La Haie Sainte

Donzelot

La Belle Alliance

Quiot

Collaert

Kielmansegge

Lambert

Ompteda

Milhaud

Somerset

Lefebvre Desnouëttes

Kellerman

Guyot

Collaert

von Kruse

Arentsschildt

Chassé

Foy

du Plat

Halkett

Jérôme

Merbe Braine

Detmers

Brunswickers

W Halkett

Adam

Grant

Mon Plaisir

Mitchell

Piré

Hougoumont

Braine l'Alleud

Varral

Pospol

N

Bradt

1000m

1000yds

The weapons of the Napoleonic Wars caused atrocious wounds. Cannonballs were capable of taking a man's head clean off; canister (grapeshot) and musket balls would shatter limbs and smash into soft tissue. The artillery caused most wounds, mainly to legs. The prime treatment for damaged limbs was amputation, with a saw, with the victim held down by orderlies. A tourniquet was applied to shut off the blood supply, severed arteries were tied with thread, a flap of skin was sewn over the stump, then bandaged. There was no anaesthetic – that was first introduced in the 1840s – and little understanding of hygiene and infection. Nonetheless, survival rates were reasonably good: 60–75% for amputated legs, for instance. Musket balls and shrapnel could be extracted by forceps, and it was vital also to remove shredded uniform cloth and mud that entered the body with them, to prevent gangrene. Serious wounds to the abdomen tended to be fatal. The French were rather more advanced in battlefield medicine on account of the pioneering work of Dominique-Jean Larrey (1766–1842), Chief Surgeon to the French army from 1797 to 1815, who was present at Waterloo. He recognised that speed of treatment was a key factor in recovery, and so did everything to get wounded men off the battlefield as soon as possible. One of his contributions was the ambulance: a light carriage with a stretcher, attended by trained crews. Surgeons worked for days after the Battle of Waterloo, treating thousands of wounded men. One of these was the 21-year-old Louis-Joseph Seutin (1793–1862), a Belgian doctor who had formerly served under Larrey in the French army. At Waterloo he was a surgeon for the Anglo-Allied forces, working in an improvised field station where he carried out 32 amputations in a day. Later he became famous as the father of plaster-cast bone-setting.

battle at Wavre, trying to dislodge Prussians from houses and bridges along the river Dyle. The orders that had reached Grouchy had been so ambiguous that he decided to hold the Prussians in Wavre, but he was only engaging the rearguard: he had let slip 48,000 Prussians. Now General Friedrich Bülow's IV Corps were heading through woods towards Plancenoit, 1.5km to the southeast of La Belle Alliance – threatening to outflank Napoleon's right, to attack his headquarters at Rossomme, and to cut off his army's retreat. At the same time a northern column under Lieutenant General Hans von Ziethen was closing in the Ferme de la Papelotte, from where they would be able to reinforce Wellington's lines. When the Prussians succeeded in taking Plancenoit at 18.00, Napoleon was obliged to dispatch 2,000 of his precious Young Guard (from his Imperial Guard reserves) to retake it, and brutal hand-to-hand street fighting ensued. To win the day, Napoleon now needed to deliver a crushing blow to Wellington.

At 18.30, Marshal Ney attacked the Anglo-Allied right and centre, this time with a more conventional force of infantry backed by artillery and cavalry. All day a 400-strong contingent of the King's German Legion had been defending the Ferme de la Haie Sainte. Now they ran out of ammunition and were overwhelmed; only 42 survived. So the farm – just yards from Wellington's centre, fell into French hands. The failure of Wellington to resupply the farm was deemed at the time to have been Wellington's greatest mistake of the battle. The Prince of Orange then compounded the loss by misguidedly endorsing an order to send a battalion of the King's German Legion under the Hanoverian Colonel Christian von Ompteda to retake the farm, only to be annihilated by French cavalry. The French now used the Ferme de la Haie Sainte to launch attacks on the Anglo-Allied centre, sending skirmishers up the hill and bringing up three horse artillery cannon to blast away at Wellington's lines. Meanwhile Durutte was on the verge of taking Papelotte to the east. A French infantry division, led by Lieutenant Generals Gilbert Bachelu and Maximilien Foy, was attacking Wellington's right; D'Erlon renewed his assault on the left. These were desperate times: Wellington was staring defeat in the face. He sent the regimental colours to the rear for safekeeping, a sure sign that the battle was in the balance. But now the Prussians were renewing pressure on Plancenoit; Ziethen's column was coming in from the east. Wellington just needed to hold on. He rallied his troops and Bachelu and Foy were repulsed.

French foot soldiers fighting in close formation at a re-enactment show the vulnerability of infantry to artillery fire (© Joseph Jeanmart/Whybelgium.co.uk)

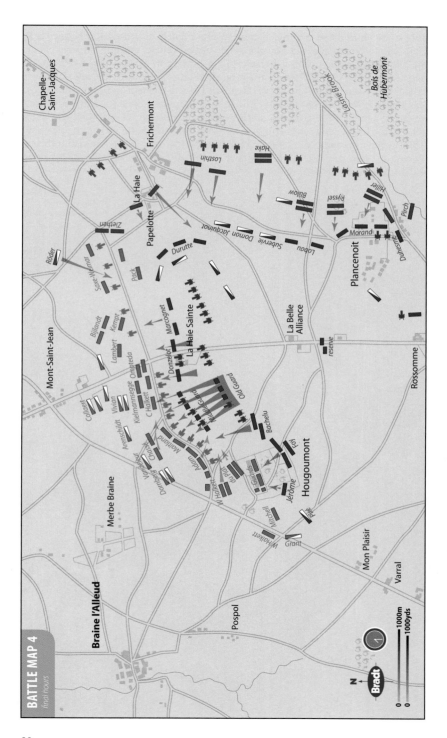

Chapelle-
Saint-Jacques

Frichermont

Bois de
Hubermont

Lost
hin

Lasne Brook

Hake

La Haie

Bülow

Hiller

Papelotte

Ryssel

Pirch

Ziethen

Morand

Röder

Lobau

Subervie Domon Jacquinot

Duhesme

Durutte

Plancenoit

Saxe-Weimar

Pack

Mont-Saint-Jean

Bijlandt

Marcognet

reserve

Kempt

La Haie Sainte

La Belle
Alliance

Lambert

Donzelot

Rossomme

Colleert

Ompteda

Middle Guard

Vivian

Kielmannsegge

Old Guard

Arenschildt

C Halkett

Bachelu

Vordeleur

Chassé

Maitland

Foy

Merbe Braine

Domberg

Adam

du Plat

Guards

Hougoumont

W Halkett

Jérôme

Mitchell

Piré

Mon Plaisir

Whitlett

Grant

Varral

Braine l'Alleud

Pospol

N

Bradt

0
0
1000m
1000yds

28

DEFEAT OF THE IMMORTALS Now Napoleon sent in the Imperial Guard – 'the Immortals'. He led the Middle Guard out beyond La Belle Alliance, then stood aside to let them pass and receive their cheers: *'Vive l'Empereur!'* They headed towards Wellington's right and centre. The Dutch–Belgian horse artillery, Wellington's last reserves, brought up their guns, firing wave after wave of canister, filling the air with smoke. Yet the Guards marched on, climbing over the bodies of their fallen comrades, picking their way around fallen horses. The British and Allied troops formed lines four deep, staying low and holding fire until the French columns came within 25m. Then they stood up and they unleashed withering fire. The 52nd Regiment of Foot Guards under Lieutenant Colonel Sir John Colborne came out of line and poured devastating enfilading fire into the left flank of the columns. Now Dutch–Belgian troops led by Lieutenant General David Chassé weighed in decisively, and the Anglo-Allied lines, with fixed bayonets, rushed the French who fell back, shocked at the sheer weight of numbers that opposed them. Wellington saw the moment had come. He waved his hat three times to signal a mass attack. The Anglo-Allied forces – cavalry and infantry – ploughed into the French, cutting them down, turning their retreat into a rout.

Napoleon mounted a horse and headed down a road packed with carriages, carts and the wounded towards Charleroi. Meanwhile some of the Old Guard formed a final square just to the south of La Belle Alliance. Invited to surrender, their commander reportedly shouted defiantly *'La Garde meurt, elle ne se rend pas!'* ('The Guard dies, it does not surrender!'), or perhaps he said the equally defiant *'Merde!'*, before they were mown down.

The Prussians had poured into the French right flank, retaking Papelotte and the Ferme de la Haie and Plancenoit. Now they drove on in pursuit of Napoleon. In the late evening Blücher met Wellington at La Belle Alliance by chance and they greeted each other as victors. *'Mein lieber Kamerad,'* said Blücher. *'Quelle affaire!'*

On the battlefield before them lay most of the 48,000 wounded and 10,000 dead. Many of the wounded lay for three or more days before they were carried off; some 4,000 would die of their wounds. Their packs were looted by scavengers; many of the bodies were stripped of their uniforms. The Anglo-Allied dead were buried in mass graves, along with the horses. Many of the French were cremated on huge pyres.

On the night of 18 June, Wellington returned to his headquarters in the coaching inn at Waterloo to write his Victory Dispatch, which reached London, along with the captured eagles, to huge public acclaim on 21 June. But for Wellington there was little joy. Many of his close staff were dead or wounded; his aide-de-camp Alexander Gordon lay dying of a hip wound and amputation in Wellington's own bed. He was shocked and moved by the destruction that the battle had wrought. Later he wrote: 'Next to a battle lost, the greatest misery is a battle gained.'

ST HELENA Back in France, Napoleon – ever the optimist as well as opportunist – hoped to rally his remaining forces and fight off an Allied invasion. But after some further skirmishes it was clear that his nation had had enough. Retreating from Paris, which surrendered to the Allies on 3 July, he went to the port of Rochefort in southwest France in the hope of getting a passage to the United States of America. In the end, on 15 July 1815, he surrendered to the British, who were blockading the port. On 7 August, off the coast of Devon in England, he was put aboard HMS *Northumberland*, bound for St Helena in the far South Atlantic, where he lived resentfully, but in some comfort, until his death in 1821. He might have counted himself lucky: Marshal Ney was tried for treason by his fellow countrymen and executed by firing squad in December 1815.

The town's name is of Dutch/Flemish origin, and means 'wet forest clearing' – a clearing in the great Forêt de Soignes which stretches to the northeast to this day. The battle took place some 4km to the south of Waterloo, but Wellington set up his headquarters here, from where he sent his Victory Dispatch, and so this was the name given to the battle. Other names were used. The French called it the Battle of Mont-Saint-Jean, and the Prussians the Battle of the Belle Alliance. There are some 50 places around the (English-speaking) world named after the battle, in Canada, the Caribbean, Africa, Australia and New Zealand, and no fewer than 32 in the USA. A new bridge across the Thames in London was named Waterloo Bridge in 1815, and the area took on that name, and hence also the railway station, which opened in 1848. Waterloo may also have entered common parlance as the jocular origin of the English colloquial term for a toilet: instead of 'water closet' (the usual Victorian term for the flushing variety), 'Waterloo', or just 'loo'. ABBA's famous song 'Waterloo' (1974) is about the expression 'meeting (or facing) one's Waterloo', meaning ultimate defeat – but it is historically wrong: at Waterloo Napoleon did not surrender.

Wellington likewise was adopted as a place name for about 40 towns and cities around the world, including the capital of New Zealand. The common term for a rubber boot is named after Wellington's distinctive leather 'half-boot'. However, the origin of the name of Beef Wellington (beef in a pastry crust) appears to be recent and is much less certain.

Enduring memories: (clockwise from top left) Wellington, New Zealand (© Dhoxax/Shutterstock. com); yellow wellington boots (© 79mtk/Shutterstock.com); Waterloo Village, New Jersey (© Eduard Moldoveanu/Shutterstock.com); Wellington Arch, London (© Dan Breckwoldt/Shutterstock.com)

3

The Guide

ORIENTATION

The Battle of Waterloo took place on farmland about 4km to the south of the town of Waterloo. Almost all the main sights lie along the central axis created by the N5 Brussels–Charleroi road, or close to it. This includes the Musée Wellington (Wellington's headquarters) in Waterloo Town; the Ferme de Mont-Saint-Jean (brewery and military hospital museum); the main battlefield site at the Hameau du Lion, with the Memorial of the Battle of Waterloo visitor centre, Panorama and Butte du Lion (Lion Mound); the Ferme de la Belle Alliance, which stood at the centre of the French lines; and the Ferme du Caillou (Napoleon's headquarters). The Ferme de Hougoumont is the only attraction of the main battlefield that lies off this axis: it stands 1km to the west of the N5. The village of Plancenoit, where the Prussians attacked the French right flank, is 1.5km to the southeast of La Belle Alliance.

The same N5 road leads to the crossroads of Quatre-Bras, scene of the earlier battle, two days before Waterloo, between Anglo-Allied forces under Wellington and the French. Some 10km to the southeast of there is Ligny, where Napoleon defeated the Prussians that same day.

All these sights are within 25 km of the town of Waterloo – as indeed are the recommended excursions to Nivelles, the Abbaye de Villers, Louvain-la-Neuve and Wavre (Walibi and Aventure Parc).

THE MAIN SITES

THE BATTLEFIELD

Hameau du Lion The 'Hamlet of the Lion' is the centrepiece of the battlefield, where visitor attractions cluster at the foot of the huge Butte du Lion, the 'Lion Mound'. It is not in fact at the centre of the original battlefield: the original central axis was the Brussels–Charleroi road, 400m to the east, which ran between the crossroads where Wellington stationed himself to the inn of La Belle Alliance on the other side of the shallow valley, which stood in the middle of the French lines. But ever since the Butte du Lion was completed in 1826, the Hameau du Lion has been the first port of call for battlefield tourists. Over the years it acquired a 'hamlet' of privately owned museums, lodgings and restaurants of mixed merit. As the bicentenary of the Battle of Waterloo approached, the Walloon regional and local authorities realised that improvements were needed, and gradually brought the site into the public domain. It then came up with a radical plan that swept almost all of the old hamlet away, to be replaced by a new complex: the cutting-edge sunken visitor centre and an above-ground catering and hospitality building in the original early 19th-century style.

Memorial of the Battle of Waterloo visitor centre (⏱ *Apr–Sep 09.30–18.30 daily, Oct–Mar 10.00–17.00 daily; for contact details & admission prices, see*

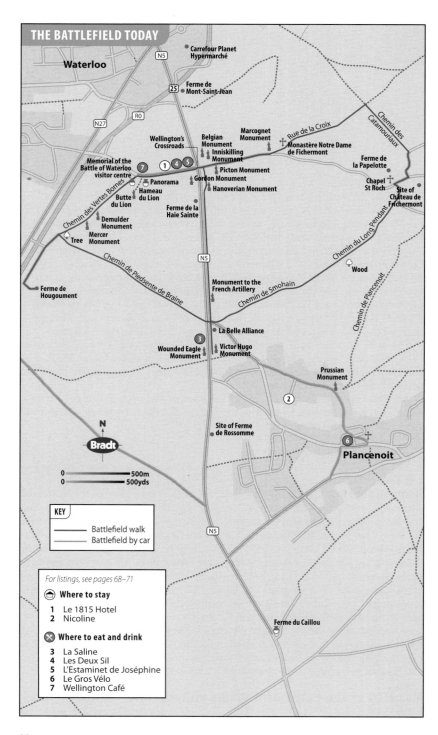

THE BATTLEFIELD TODAY

Waterloo

Carrefour Planet
Hypermarché

N5

Ferme de
Mont-Saint-Jean

25

N27

R0

Wellington's
Crossroads

Belgian
Monument

Marcognet
Monument

Rue de la Croix

Chemin des Catamouriaux

Memorial of the
Battle of Waterloo
visitor centre

Inniskilling
Monument

Monastère Notre Dame
de Fichermont

Ferme de
la Papelotte

7   1   4   5

Picton Monument

Chemin des Vertes Bornes

Panorama

Gordon Monument

Chapel
St Roch

Site of
Château de
Fichermont

Hameau
du Lion

Hanoverian Monument

Butte
du Lion

Ferme de la
Haie Sainte

Demulder
Monument

Mercer
Monument

Chemin du Long Pendant

Tree

Chemin de Piedsente de Braine

N5

Ferme de
Hougoument

Monument to the
French Artillery

Wood

Chemin de Smohain

Chemin de Plancenoit

La Belle Alliance

3

Wounded Eagle
Monument

Victor Hugo
Monument

Prussian
Monument

2

N

Bradt

Site of Ferme
de Rossomme

6

Plancenoit

0 ──────── 500m
0 ──────── 500yds

KEY

Battlefield walk
Battlefield by car

N5

Ferme du Caillou

The 4D cinema experience at the new Memorial of the Battle of Waterloo visitor centre (© La Belle Alliance)

www.visitwaterloo.be) This new interpretation centre opening in May 2015, will be striking in its underground construction, designed to minimise its impact on the battle sightlines. Using new technologies in museum presentation and immersive 'scenography' (by means of lighting, sound and set-design), it will offer a background and context to the Battle of Waterloo, from the French Revolution to the lead-up to the battle, and the bivouacs the preceding night. A film by the respected Belgian director Gérard Corbiau in 4D (3D plus physical effects, such as smell and the shuddering ground), will be presented on a large semicircular screen, and will 'put the visitor inside the battle'. Finally, the visitor will be shown the outcome of the battle: the human toll, the celebrations of the victors, and the consequences for Europe. A tunnel leads to the Panorama and the Butte du Lion.

Panorama This is a piece of history in itself: a colossal oil painting, 12m high, 110m long, inside a rotunda, and entirely encircling a central viewing plinth. The scene is Marshal Ney's cavalry charge on the Anglo-Allied squares, and it is as if you the visitor are in the square. It is impressive now, and it must have been even more impressive to viewers when it was first opened in 1912, at the tail-end of the popular vogue for such ambitious panorama paintings. Created by the French artist Louis Dumoulin (1860–1924) and a team of assistants nearly 100 years after the battle, and over 100 years ago, it stands as a monument to the public's enduring fascination for the battle.

Butte du Lion The 'Mound of the Lion' is the most prominent feature of the landscape, essentially the emblem of the battlefield, visible for miles around. With a viewing platform 43m above its base, accessed by a narrow stone staircase of 226

A 28-tonne Royal Dutch lion crowns the plinth at the top of the Butte du Lion (© WBT/JL Flémal)

The Ferme de Hougoumont lay some 400m in front of the Anglo-Allied lines (© Antony Mason)

steps, it is a good place to survey the battlefield, so it repays bringing a map with you. The huge cast-iron lion, a Dutch royal symbol denoting courage, stands atop its stone plinth looking defiantly towards France. The Butte du Lion was always a controversial monument. Erected by the Dutch in 1823–26 on the orders of King William I of the Netherlands (which then included Belgium), it marks the spot where his son and heir, 22-year-old Prince William of Orange was wounded by a musket ball to the shoulder – strange that the biggest monument on a field where 10,000 died recalls the wound of a young, inexperienced and impetuous commander, whom Wellington was forced for diplomatic reasons to accept, and who did not acquit himself well. The Dutch (who ruled Belgium to 1830) employed thousands of labourers to scrape nearly 400,000 cubic metres of soil from the surrounding landscape, flattening the high banks of the 'sunken roads' which played such an important role in the battle, and unearthing numerous hastily buried bodies. It is said that, when Wellington saw the mound two years after its completion, he proclaimed, 'They have ruined my battlefield.' The French meanwhile resented the monument as an expression of triumphalism. That said, it is a bold and distinctive landmark, without which the battlefield might seem mundane.

FERME DE HOUGOUMONT (*1 Chemin de Hougoumont, 1420 Braine-l'Alleud; for contact details, opening times & admission prices, see www.visitwaterloo.be*) Sometimes also called Goumont (its original name until the 18th century), Hougoumont is also referred to as a *ferme-château* because that is what it was until the battle: a grand, if small-scale 17th-century manor house with a walled formal garden and orchard, and a working farm attached. The Battle of Waterloo began here, at around 11.30, as French troops of Lieutenant General Reille's II Corps, led by Napoleon's brother Prince Jérôme, attacked through woods (since gone) to the south, confronting Nassauer and Hanoverian troops stationed in the garden and orchard and British Coldstream and Scots guards (Foot Guards, as they are referred to on a plaque) in the farm and château. Although the assault continued all day, and the château was destroyed by fire caused by shelling, the French never succeeded in dislodging its defenders (reinforced and resupplied from the lines to their rear – notably by Private Brewer driving an ammunition cart to the door under intense fire, as commemorated by another plaque). At one point a contingent of about 40 French infantrymen, led by a giant called Sous-Lieutenant Legros, wielding an axe, burst through the north gate, but British soldiers, including the garrison commander Lieutenant Colonel James Macdonnell, managed to close the door behind them to keep others out: all the French were then slaughtered, apart from a drummer boy. Because of the strategic importance of Hougoumont, Wellington remarked 'the success of the

The battlefield of Waterloo became a tourist attraction immediately after the battle. Soon, British visitors were coming from London by stagecoaches organised by the forerunners of modern tour operators, and facilities were built to accommodate them. After 1826, they had the Butte du Lion to admire. Sergeant Major Edward Cotton (1792–1849), who had fought at the battle with the 7th Hussars, became a local innkeeper and battlefield guide, and created the first battlefield museum in the 1830s (its contents were sold by auction in 1909 and dispersed around the world). The old Hôtel du Musée at the Hameau du Lion was opened in 1857; this was one of a cluster of old and rather decrepit buildings that was cleared away for the new battlefield Visitor Centre prior to 2015.

battle turned upon closing the gates at Hougoumont'. This event is the inspiration behind the magnificent new bronze sculpture, featuring two British solders, by Vivien Mallock, which won the Project Hougoumont competition for a commememorative monument for 2015. What is left of the complex – the farm buildings, chapel and the old gardener's house – has been undergoing renovation (without rebuilding what was lost during the battle, or demolished after it), with one of the barns housing an interpretation centre to explain events here due to open in June 2015. The tiny chapel was famous for its large statue of Christ on the cross, with its feet burnt off by the fire – mentioned by Victor Hugo in *Les Misérables*. This was stolen in 2011, but was fortunately recovered in 2014. The former walled garden, now a paddock, contains a number of memorials, including a stone monument erected in 1912, topped by an imperial eagle, to the French (some 4,000 of them) who died at Hougoumont. South of the garden wall (still pierced by loopholes pushed out by the defenders) lay an open gap before the woods, the 'killing field': a plaque on the wall commemorates Brigadier General Pierre-François Bauduin, the first general to die at Waterloo.

FERME DE MONT-SAINT-JEAN (*591 Chaussée de Charleroi, 1410 Waterloo; for contact details, opening times & admission prices, see www.visitwaterloo.be*) The name recalls the fact that this was once a farm belonging to the Knights of St John (Knights of Malta); the first mention of this appears in 1358. The current building dates from 1719, and has the high arched carriage entrance that is typical of Brabançon farmhouses. Wellington slept here for three hours on the night of 17 June, before the battle. Being behind the Anglo-Allied lines, on the road to Brussels, it was well placed to serve as a military hospital, and did so for four days during and after the battle. Some 6,000 wounded men passed through here, including the Prince of Orange, as amputated limbs piled up in the courtyard corners. It has recently been

Commemorating the British: the clay maquette for Vivien Mallock's bronze sculpture installed at Hougoumont in 2015 (© Vivien Mallock)

undergoing renovation under the direction of Anthony Martin of the Brasserie de Waterloo (and part of the family firm that runs the Martin's Hotel group) with two goals: to become a microbrewery producing the Waterloo brand of beer, with accompanying brasserie-restaurant, and also to present a museum about the 'English Hospital'.

FERME DU CAILLOU (*66 Chaussée de Bruxelles, 1472 Vieux-Genappe;* ✆ *02 384 24 24; www.visitwaterloo.be;* ⊕ *Apr–Sep 9.30–18.00 daily, Oct–Mar 10.00–17.00 daily; adult/child 7–17 €4/€3*) Napoleon's last HQ (Dernier QG de Napoléon) lies 2.5km south of the Hameau du Lion on the N5 Brussels–Charleroi road (reachable by Bus 365a; see page 3). Here, in this old farmhouse, Napoleon and his staff spent the night of 17 June. It was set on fire by the Prussians on 19 June, the day after the Battle of Waterloo, but was rebuilt in 1818 and became a coaching inn. It is now a museum devoted to Napoleon, his staff and army, with weapons, decorations, medals, correspondence, paintings, engravings and maps. It also has a few very personal mementos of Napoleon, including a lock of his hair and his camp bed. In advance of the bicentenary, the museum was completely overhauled, updated and rethought, with a new audioguide-led presentation. Outside, in the garden, is a small brick ossuary, built in 1912 to contain miscellaneous battlefield bones. The neighbouring walled orchard is where the *Grognards* (literally 'grumblers') of the Old Guard bivouacked to keep watch. In the approach to the museum is an unusual modern bronze statue of Napoleon (2010), depicting the moment when he realised that the battle was lost.

La Ferme de la Haie Sainte is still a private, working farm (© Antony Mason)

BATTLE BUILDINGS NOT OPEN TO THE PUBLIC
Ferme de la Haie Sainte Also spelled Haye Sainte, the name seems to mean 'sacred hedge', but Sainte referred to the family name of the owners. The farm, and its adjacent garden to the north and orchard to the south, stood right in the middle of the Anglo-Allied lines, just below the ridge, in front of Wellington's elm tree. This was one of the three improvised fortresses of Wellington's line, defended initially by 400 riflemen of the King's German Legion (KGL) led by Major George Baring, later reinforced by about 400 Nassauers. It had not been properly prepared and barricaded for this role – indeed, soldiers spending the night of 17 June there burnt the farm gates for firewood (the gateway was later blocked off by bodies). The French battled all day to take it, but the defenders doggedly fought them off until about 18.30, after they had run out of ammunition. In a mêlée of hand-to-hand fighting, Baring was reduced to throwing roof tiles at the enemy from the pigsty roof, while Ensign Frank, hiding under a bed in the attack, watched two wounded

EYEWITNESS ACCOUNT

Rees Howell Gronow (1794–1865) was a 21-year-old Guards officer at Waterloo. Having joined the British army in 1813, he had served under the Duke of Wellington in Spain, and fought at Quatre-Bras. His vivid account of the Battle of Waterloo appeared in his memoir The Reminiscences of Captain Gronow *(1862).*

During the battle our squares presented a shocking sight. Inside we were nearly suffocated by the smoke and smell from burnt cartridges. It was impossible to move a yard without treading upon a wounded comrade, or upon the bodies of the dead; and the loud groans of the wounded and dying were most appalling.

At four o'clock our square was a perfect hospital, being full of dead, dying, and mutilated soldiers. The charges of cavalry were in appearance very formidable, but in reality a great relief, as the artillery could no longer fire on us: the very earth shook under the enormous mass of men and horses. I never shall forget the strange noise our bullets made against the breastplates of Kellermann's and Milhaud's Cuirassiers, six or seven thousand in number, who attacked us with great fury. I can only compare it, with a somewhat homely simile, to the noise of a violent hail-storm beating upon panes of glass.

The artillery did great execution, but our musketry did not at first seem to kill many men; though it brought down a large number of horses, and created indescribable confusion. The horses of the first rank of Cuirassiers, in spite of all the efforts of their riders, came to a stand-still, shaking and covered with foam, at about twenty yards' distance from our squares, and generally resisted all attempts to force them to charge the line of serried steel. On one occasion, two gallant French officers forced their way into a gap momentarily created by the discharge of artillery: one was killed by [Colonel] Staples, the other by [Captain] Adair. Nothing could be more gallant than the behaviour of those veterans, many of whom had distinguished themselves on half the battlefields of Europe.

In the midst of our terrible fire, their officers were seen as if on parade, keeping order in their ranks, and encouraging them. Unable to renew the charge, but unwilling to retreat, they brandished their swords with loud cries of *'Vive l'Empereur!'* and allowed themselves to be mowed down by hundreds rather than yield. Our men, who shot them down, could not help admiring the gallant bearing and heroic resignation of their enemies.

comrades being bayoneted to death. Only 42 of the KGL garrison, including Baring, managed to escape back to the Anglo-Allied lines. Remarkably unchanged since 1815, La Haie Sainte is still a working farm, and only the exterior can be seen. The wall overlooking the busy N5 Brussels–Charleroi road bears four plaques (commemorating the KGL, Major Baring and Colonel von Ompteda (see page 26), the taking of the farm by the French under Marshal Ney, and to the French troops who fell here), but they are hard to approach because of the busy road.

La Belle Alliance

La Belle Alliance   In 1815, this house on the Brussels–Charleroi road was an inn as well as a farm, built in the 1760s. The central part of the building (with the door and windows) looks today more or less as it did then; the barn attached to the north is a more recent extension. La Belle Alliance stands in the centre of the ridge defended by the French, with good views across most of the valley. It was not Napoleon's battle headquarters – that was a viewpoint on a hillock (the view is now obscured) beside a farmhouse at Rossomme (destroyed by fire in 1895), 1km down the road to the south – but La Belle Alliance was a rallying point for his commanders, the equivalent of Wellington's elm tree at the crossroads on the other side of the valley. Napoleon however came to it several times: on the night before the battle, and in the morning to review his troops as they marched to their positions. He also came here to lead in the final assault by the Imperial Guard. All the while, La Belle Alliance served as a field hospital, where scores of French casualties were treated by the French Medical Corps – as a plaque on the wall attests. Another plaque commemorates the chance meeting here of Wellington and Blücher on the evening of the battle when they greeted each other as mutual victors – the occasion when Blücher made the famous understatement: '*Mein lieber Kamerad! Quelle affaire!*' The name of the building does not refer to the battle alliance, but to a previous marriage between the landowner and one of her farmhands. It is now a nightclub.

La Belle Alliance (painted white, just right of centre), viewed across the battlefield from close to Wellington's crossroads (© Antony Mason)

La Ferme de la Papelotte today is part of a tranquil little hamlet (© Antony Mason)

Ferme de la Papelotte This large farm is the only survivor among a set of buildings that formed the end point of Wellington's left (the Ferme de la Haie and the Château de Frichermont (see page 49) have been demolished). It was defended by Nassauer troops (under the overall command of Prince Bernhard of Saxe-Weimar at the head of a Netherlands Brigade) during D'Erlon's first major offensive of the battle, and came under constant attack from skirmishers until, late in the day, a full attack by French troops under Durutte nearly secured it, but the French were forced finally to retreat by the Prussians under Ziethen. Badly damaged in the fighting, it was remodelled in the late 19th century (with a tower over the entrance). Today it is a private riding centre.

3

MARSHAL BLÜCHER

Field Marshal Gebhard Leberecht von Blücher (1742–1819) was 72 at the Battle of Waterloo. Commander-in-Chief of the Prussian army, he was – despite his age – known as an energetic and unstoppable force: his nickname was 'Marschall Vorwärts' (Marshal Forwards). A cavalry general, by 1815 he was celebrated above all for his part in the decisive defeat of Napoleon at the Battle of Leipzig in 1813. He was also violent and vengeful and had an irascible relationship with superior authority, and beneath his bluster lay a history of mental frailty: in 1806–09 he had had a mental breakdown in which – among other disturbing illusions – he was convinced he was pregnant with an elephant. His unyielding determination to assist Wellington to defeat Napoleon and the French, whom he detested with a passion, was sufficient to overcome the initial setbacks at Ligny and to provide crucial assistance at a critical time at Waterloo. Badly bruised at Ligny after being trapped under his fallen horse, he arrived at Waterloo stinking of an ointment made of brandy, gin, garlic and rhubarb, which amused him. He adored his troops, whom he addressed as 'my children', and the affection was returned by their courage and loyalty.

LORD UXBRIDGE'S LEG

A curiosity of the Musée Wellington is Lord Uxbridge's false leg. In a famous incident of the Battle of Waterloo, close to the end, Henry Paget, Lord Uxbridge, commander of the Anglo-Allied cavalry, had his leg shattered by grapeshot while riding beside Wellington. Uxbridge, famed for his stiff upper lip, said, 'By God, sir, I have lost my leg!' to which Wellington replied, 'By God, sir, so you have!' Uxbridge's leg was later amputated, and he survived and lived as the newly created Marquis of Anglesey, until 1854. The amputated leg was buried in its own grave at Waterloo, with a gravestone, in the garden of the house where the operation took place, and this became a tourist attraction. It was later dug up and exhibited in the house until 1878 when Uxbridge's son came to Waterloo and, horrified, demanded that the bones be returned to England. Quite what happened after this is disputed. One story relates that, instead of being repatriated, they were hidden by the owner of the house, and eventually incinerated in 1934. Another says that they were reburied in the grounds of the Musée Wellington in 1991. Meanwhile, in a case within the museum, you can see one of Lord Uxbridge's prosthetic legs.

Wellington's headquarters at the centre of the town of Waterloo is now a museum (© Antony Mason)

WATERLOO TOWN

Musée Wellington (*147 Chaussée de Bruxelles, 1410 Waterloo;* ✎ *02 357 28 60; www.museewellington.be;* ⊕ *Apr–Sep 09.30–18.00 daily, Oct–Mar 10.00–17.00 daily; adult/student/child 7–17 €6.50/€5.50/€4*) The Wellington Museum is the former Brabant coaching inn where Wellington and his staff stayed on the nights of 17 and 18 June 1815, and so this was effectively his headquarters. Here, too, he wrote his Victory Dispatch, as his aide-de-camp Colonel Sir Alexander Gordon, after having his leg amputated, died in his (Wellington's) bed in the adjacent room. Given this story, and the authentic feel to the rooms in this old inn (built in around 1705), this is an atmospheric place, filled with mementos of the battle, and of both Wellington and Napoleon: paintings, weapons, uniforms, decorations, and letters. With the help of an audioguide, progressing through the rooms also takes you through the various stages of the battle, with maps – a concise and useful introduction. A new wing at the back presents a broader picture of war in general, and also holds temporary exhibitions.

Chapelle Royale and Eglise Saint-Joseph (*Pl Albert 1er, 1410 Waterloo; http://sjoseph.be;* ⊕ *08.00–19.00 daily; free*) The grand, domed building opposite the Musée Wellington is the Chapelle Royale, built in Baroque style in 1687–90 during the rule of the Spanish Netherlands by the then Governor General, the Marquis of Castanaga, in the hope that this gesture would produce a male heir for King Charles II of Spain (it didn't). At the time it was an imposing monument in a tiny hamlet on a busy transit road. It was deconsecrated by the French Revolutionary Army in the 1790s. After 1815, it became a kind of shrine to the fallen at the Battle of Waterloo. Inside, beneath the cupola, is a fine marble bust of Wellington, made in 1855 (three years after his death): you can see here why he was nicknamed 'Old Nosey' by his troops. Beyond, through double doors, is the Eglise Saint-Joseph, a more conventional church inaugurated in 1824 and extended in the 1850s. At the back of the church are a number of plaques commemorating the fallen at Waterloo of all sides – affectionate monuments of loss, some of which show how Waterloo, for some, was the final battle after a long career at war. For example: 'Sacred to the memory of Colonel Sir Henry Walton Ellis KCB late of the 23rd Royal Welch Fusiliers, who after serving with distinction in Egypt, America, the West Indies, and throughout the Peninsular War, fell gallantly at the head of his Regiment on the Plains of Waterloo in the 32nd year of his age.'

Musée de Waterloo (*Waterloo Tourist Office, 218 Chaussée de Bruxelles, 1410 Waterloo;* ✎ *02 352 09 10; www.visitwaterloo.be;* ⊕ *Jun–Sep 09.30–18.00 daily, Oct–May 10.00–17.00 daily; free*) Above the Tourist Office there is a small museum dedicated not so much to the battle as to the town itself, which developed fast after 1815 on the back of battlefield tourism and industrialisation. It includes a miscellany of historic artefacts and pictures, including mementos of Victor Hugo, who visited Waterloo in 1861 and wrote about the battle in *Les Misérables*; details of the sugar factory (now the Martin's Grand Hotel), first built in 1837 and drawing on local sugar-beet production; artefacts relating to local soap and candle production (from 1872); and pictures

of the celebrated *paveurs* of Waterloo who laid the road cobbles. The museum also preserves the study of King Leopold III (reigned 1934–51) from the Château d'Argenteuil, just to the east of Waterloo, where he lived from 1961 (after his abdication) to his death in 1983; his second wife Lilian Baels (Princesse de Rethy) lived on there until her death in 2002.

THE MAIN BATTLEFIELD MONUMENTS

AT WELLINGTON'S CROSSROADS

Gordon Monument A large truncated column, symbol of a life cut short, stands to the southwest of the crossroads. This is a memorial to Colonel Sir Alexander Gordon of the 3rd Foot Guards, a veteran of the Peninsular War and a close friend of Wellington who died aged 29. One of Wellington's eight aides-de-camp, he was wounded by a cannonball to the hip when rallying British and Brunswicker troops under pressure from the Middle Guard towards the end of the battle. He underwent amputation, but died in Wellington's bed at his Waterloo headquarters (now the Musée Wellington). This monument was the first to be erected on the battlefield, in 1817.

The Gordon Monument (© Antony Mason)

Monument to the Belgians Quite how many Belgians fought at the Battle of Waterloo is unclear, as Belgium did not exist as a country until 1830, and in 1815 they were citizens of the newly created Kingdom of the Netherlands. Estimates suggest that some 4,000–6,000 Belgians took part, on both sides. A large number of Belgians had happily signed up to join the French army after their 'liberation' from Austrian rule in 1794, and fought in Napoleon's campaigns. Some rejoined Napoleon after his escape from Elba; others, however, were deeply disenchanted with the oppressive French occupation of Belgium, which in addition had failed to deliver independence, and so they joined the Anglo-Allied forces. They suffered a high number of casualties, including General Jean-Antoine de Collaert: born in Liège in 1761, he joined the hussars (light cavalry) of the Batavian Republic, a Dutch satellite allied to France, then in 1815 became commander of the cavalry

The Monument to the Belgians (© Antony Mason)

of the Kingdom of the Netherlands. Severely wounded at Waterloo, he died a year later. This monument honours the Belgians who died 'fighting for the defence of the flag and the honour of arms', thus carefully avoiding saying which side they were fighting on. It was designed to commemorate the centenary in 1915, but, poignantly, was hurriedly inaugurated in 1914, just as World War I began.

Hanoverian Monument This large, elegant, tapering block of local bluestone (limestone) was erected in 1818 to commemorate the dead of the 11,000 Hanoverians who fought with the Anglo-Allied forces. The British king, George III, was also the ruler of the German state of Hanover, although Napoleon had annexed it in 1803 – hence there was a grudge to bear. The monument is engraved with the names of 42 Anglo-German officers buried nearby. It is believed to stand on the site of a mass grave where perhaps 4,000 bodies from both sides are buried, as well as scores of horses.

Inniskilling Monument This gravestone-sized, rough-hewn stele of granite, with a

The Inniskilling Monument records the regiment's colossal casualties (© Antony Mason)

bronze plaque, was erected in 1990, in memory of the 'heroic stand' by the Irish 27th (Inniskilling) Regiment of Foot, who formed a square near here after the Ferme de la Haie Sainte fell at 18.30. The inscription goes on to say that 'of the 747 officers and men of the regiment who joined battle, 493 were killed or wounded... Of them the Duke of Wellington said, "Ah, they saved the centre of my line."'

Picton Monument This small stone stele with a bronze plaque was erected in 1980 near the spot where General Sir Thomas Picton, commander of Wellington's left wing, is believed to have been killed by a musket ball to the head during D'Erlon's attack. He was 56 years old, a veteran and hero of the Peninsular War. Already known for his eccentricity, he was wearing civilian clothes, including a top hat, and carrying an umbrella instead of a sword because of the rush to join his division. He had been

The Picton Monument, near where he fell (© Antony Mason)

wounded at Quatre-Bras but kept this from everyone but his servant. Wellington called Picton 'a rough foul-mouthed devil as ever lived', but nonetheless held him in great respect, as did his men.

NEAR LA BELLE ALLIANCE
Wounded Eagle Monument (Monument français de l'Aigle blessé)
This monument to the French soldiers who lost their lives at Waterloo is perhaps the most expressive of the battlefield memorials: designed by the famous painter and sculptor Jean-Léon Gérome, better known for his Orientalist paintings, it depicts in bronze, literally, a wounded eagle, clutching a French standard as it falls. In the aftermath of the battle there had been little appetite in France to commemorate a famous defeat, so it was a long time coming, inaugurated finally in 1904 before large crowds which included many descendants of the fallen. Set about 200m south of La Belle Alliance, next to the N5 Brussels–Charleroi road, it is said to mark the site where the Old Guard formed a square to make a last stand.

Victor Hugo Monument The great French writer Victor Hugo (1802–85) was 13 at the time of the battle and played no part in it. But he came here in 1861 and wrote about it famously in his novel *Les Misérables* (1862), which he completed nearby. He was the one who came up with the often-heard, if misleading, phrase that describes Waterloo as a *'morne plaine'* ('dismal plain'), from a poem

The Wounded Eagle Monument revisits the imperial symbol adopted by Napoleon from the Romans (© Antony Mason)

of 1852, written before he had seen it for himself. This column, just to the north of the Wounded Eagle Monument, on the other side of the road, was erected in honour of this association. Work began in 1911, but was interrupted by World War I and never completed, although inaugurated in 1956: it was going to be crowned with a large Gallic rooster, symbol of France.

AT PLANCENOIT

Prussian Monument On a raised deck surrounded by railings, on the edge of the village of Plancenoit, this elegant iron monument marks the site where the Prussian artillery was lined up to bombard the French. Designed by the great Prussian architect Karl Friedrich Schinkel, and shaped like a Gothic church spire, it was erected in 1819 in honour of the 6,700 Prussians who fell at Waterloo – or La Belle Alliance, as the German inscription calls the battle, the name that Blücher preferred.

Re-enactors' tents at Waterloo. In fact for most soldiers in 1815 a bivouac (from the German bei Wacht, 'by watch') meant sleeping in the open (© Joseph Jeanmart/Whybelgium.co.uk)

4

Walks, Tours and Excursions

A WALK AROUND THE BATTLEFIELD

You can walk right around the battlefield comfortably in about three hours (this route is about 8km long, see map page 32), but you might take longer if you linger at the Ferme de Hougoumont. Many of the paths are farm tracks and muddy after rain: wear appropriate footwear. Halfway through, you have the opportunity to take a short cut back to the Hameau du Lion from La Belle Alliance, by following the N5 road straight back across the valley through the middle of the battlefield, past the Ferme de la Haie Sainte to Wellington's crossroads. The first half of the walk includes much of the best of it. But by continuing eastwards from La Belle Alliance to the Ferme de la Papelotte you get to see the full scale of the whole of the battlefield, and the entirety of the ridges along which both sides lined up to face each other. It is said that Waterloo was a relatively small battlefield, but Wellington's line nonetheless stretched from Hougoumont to Papelotte, a distance of 3.5km, along which 61,000 soldiers stood to await battle.

ANGLO-ALLIED SQUARES   Start at the Hameau du Lion (site of the new visitor centre, the Panorama and the Butte du Lion; see pages 31–4). From the Panorama head along the track called the Chemin des Vertes Bornes towards the Ferme de Hougoumont. This follows the ridge defended primarily by the King's German Legion, the Hanoverians and the British, who were battered by French artillery for much of the opening part of the battle. But you can see clearly the advantage of this position on the reverse side of the crest: they were protected from cannon fire by the crest – the French ridge on the other side of the valley is out of sight for most of the way. The Anglo-Allied artillery was lined up along the forward side of the ridge. It was along this ridge too that, at about 16.00, the Anglo-Allied infantry formed their squares to meet the relentless and ultimately fruitless attacks by the French cavalry. And it was near here that finally, at about 19.30, the Imperial Guard were repulsed.

There are two monuments along this path. The **Demulder Monument** is dedicated, unusually, to a Belgian, saying (in translation): 'To the memory of Lieutenant Augustin Demulder of the 5th Cuirassiers, born at Nivelles in Brabant in 1785, Knight of the Legion of Honour, wounded at Eylau in 1807, at Essling 1809, at Hanau 1813. Killed at Waterloo. And in memory of all the cavalry that charged with him on 18 June 1815.' Like many of his countrymen, Demulder had fought with the French since joining up in 1807, and remained loyal to Napoleon to the end. The **Mercer Monument** records the last position that Captain Alexander Cavilié Mercer's G Troop of the Royal Horse Artillery stationed their five nine-pounder guns and a howitzer, unleashing devastating and critical fire on attacking cavalry and infantry, as it had done throughout the battle. Mercer later wrote a graphic account of the battle called *Journal of the Waterloo Campaign*. He died in 1868.

Continue past the sole tree on the road, and down into the woods that lie straight ahead. This leads, after about 500m, to the **Ferme de Hougoumont** (see pages 34–5). These woods were not here at the time of the battle: instead the Anglo-Allied infantry and cavalry on the ridge had a clear view of the farm. There were, however, thick woods on the other side of the farm, through which the French mounted the first attack of the day at around 11.30. This approach to the farm shows how it stood out on a limb, and close to the French lines – so it is all the more remarkable that it held out against attack for the entire day.

Head back along the road you have just come along and turn right just before the tree; this is the Chemin de Plancenoit, which leads down into the base of the valley and becomes the Chemin de Piedsente de Braine. Ahead lies La Belle Alliance, the inn which was the command point at the centre of the French lines. The strategic advantage of its location becomes evident when you find that it is rarely out of sight throughout the rest of the tour around the battlefield. As you head down into the valley turn around to look how the tree sinks behind the ridge, demonstrating again the protective virtues of the reverse slope. You can also imagine what toil was demanded of the French cavalry and infantry to mount the hill through matted crops and thick mud. Wellington's cunning in choosing the terrain to defend becomes ever clearer.

THE CENTRE OF THE FRENCH FRONT LINE The original, central part of **La Belle Alliance** (see page 38) has changed little since 1815, but it is now a nightclub and there is nothing to visit. The precise movements of Napoleon are unclear, but he seems to have spent part of the time here, at the beginning of the battle as his troops took up position, and as he led out the Imperial Guard part of the way on their final assault; but most of the time he seems to have been at the Ferme de Rossomme (which no longer exists, having been burnt down in a fire in 1895), about 1km further south. If you cross the busy N5 road that rushes past La Belle Alliance (do take care) you can read the two plaques on the façade, one recording the encounter between Wellington and Marshal Blücher here at the end of the battle (see page 29), and the other to the French Medical Corps, who treated the wounded in this building during the battle. If you walk south along the N5, after about 150m, you come first to the **Victor Hugo Monument** (the tall pillar on the left; see pages 44–5), and then to the **Wounded Eagle Monument**, the most elaborate and anguished of the battlefield monuments (see page 44), said to mark the place where the Imperial Guard formed a square to make their last stand.

Return to La Belle Alliance, and cross the N5 to the eastern side. Here you have a choice: to continue round the full circuit of the battlefield, or to return to the Hameau du Lion.

SHORTCUT HOME **To return to the Hameau du Lion:** Head down the tarmac and concrete path that leads along the eastern side of the busy and noisy N5. After a short while the road is separated from the path by a low hedge. On the right, shortly after the hedge begins, is a simple **Monument to the French Artillery**, surmounted by an imperial eagle. It commemorates the support given by the artillery, which lined the ridge on Napoleon's right, to the I Corps under the Comte D'Erlon,

La Belle Alliance served as a field hospital
(© Antony Mason)

The Monument to the French Artillery (© Antony Mason)

who led the first major infantry attack against Wellington's left at around 13.30. Continuing on, as you head up out of the base of the valley, you come first to the Ferme de la Haie Sainte and then to the Hanoverian Memorial, the Gordon Memorial and Wellington's crossroads. (Here you join the last section of the full tour; for descriptions, see pages 50–1.) Use the pedestrian crossing at the traffic lights to cross the N5 and head back towards the Butte du Lion and the Hameau du Lion.

THE FRENCH RIGHT AND WELLINGTON'S LEFT

To continue around the battlefield: Walk along the road a little to the east of La Belle Alliance, and take

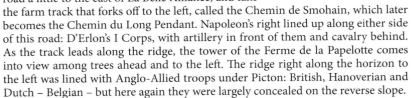

the farm track that forks off to the left, called the Chemin de Smohain, which later becomes the Chemin du Long Pendant. Napoleon's right lined up along either side of this road: D'Erlon's I Corps, with artillery in front of them and cavalry behind. As the track leads along the ridge, the tower of the Ferme de la Papelotte comes into view among trees ahead and to the left. The ridge right along the horizon to the left was lined with Anglo-Allied troops under Picton: British, Hanoverian and Dutch – Belgian – but here again they were largely concealed on the reverse slope.

The track skirts a wood, then Papelotte appears ahead before the path drops down into another wood with high banks on either side. Many of the roads on the battlefield were described as 'sunken lanes', which presented serious obstacles to troops and cavalry trying to cross them. We can imagine that this lane is how many of them looked in 1815. Turn left and north as you reach the T-junction in the woods, and continue on down to the crossroads at the foot of the hill. Ahead is a tiny chapel built in 1867, and dedicated to St Roch, a 14th-century French holy man widely invoked against disease and the plague. Beyond is the **Ferme de la Papelotte** (see page 39), much altered since the battle, and now a private riding school. In 1815, this farm was defended by Nassauer troops at the beginning of the battle. Together with the nearby **Ferme de la Haie**, or Haye, to the east (destroyed by fire in 1910), and the **Château de Frichermont** to the southeast (also spelled Fichermont; destroyed by fire in 1857 and razed in 1965), they anchored the easternmost end of Wellington's left. There is nothing now to see at the Château de Frichermont, but it is worth noting that the Duke of Marlborough made his headquarters here in 1705, during the War of the Spanish Succession, and – like Wellington – identified the valley of Mont-Saint-Jean (ie: the battlefield of Waterloo) as a good place from which to face an attack on Brussels. The French under General Durutte took the Ferme de la Haie during D'Erlon's early attack, and took the Ferme de la Papelotte temporarily twice, but they were forced to retreat by the arrival of the I Corps of the Prussians under Ziethen at about 19.30.

Turn right at the little St Roch chapel, then take the first left along the Chemin des Catamouriaux. Keep left as you pass the Chemin de la Sablonnière, and climb the long hill to the crossroads. This is the kind of incline the French troops had to deal with to reach the Anglo-Allied lines. To the right of the crossroads Ziethen received orders from Blücher via Major von Schornhorst to divert south to Plancenoit instead of heading along the ridge to support Wellington; the Prussian liaison officer attached to Wellington, Baron von Müffling, understood the danger this would pose to Wellington, now under grave threat after the fall of the Ferme de la Haie Sainte at the centre, and he managed to persuade Ziethen to go to Wellington's aid. It was one of the critical decisions that may have won the battle.

Now turn left along that ridge, following the Chemin de la Croix. Soon you come to the Monastère Notre Dame de Fichermont, a former Dominican convent, built in 1927–45 in contravention of a 1914 law protecting the battlefield; it is now occupied by another religious community called Le Verbe de Vie. A former resident here was the Singing Nun ('Soeur Sourire'), who was catapulted to fame in 1963 by her pop song 'Dominique', an international success that blighted the rest of her tragic life, which ended in suicide in 1985. Where the track meets the Rue de la Croix you will find the **Marcognet Monument**, commemorating the clash between the French infantry division led by General Pierre-Louis Binet de Marcognet and the Anglo-Scots Brigade under Major General Denis Pack, during D'Erlon's initial attack. The French infantry sensed victory, but were driven off by the famous charge of the Scots Greys Dragoons. Marcognet survived and lived to 1854.

THE CENTRE OF THE ANGLO-ALLIED LINE

Continue along the cobbled Rue de la Croix in the direction of the Butte du Lion, to reach Wellington's crossroads. The first monuments you come to, either side of the road, are two stone steles with brass plates. On the left is the **Picton Monument** (see page 44) near the spot where General Sir Thomas Picton, commander of Wellington's left wing, is believed to have been killed by a musket ball to the head during D'Erlon's attack. On the right is the **Inniskilling Monument** (see pages 43–4), honouring the fact that over half their number were killed or wounded defending the centre of the Anglo-Allied line after the fall of the Ferme de la Haie Sainte.

Take the path to the left, through the trees. This leads past the site of the gravel or sand pit (since filled in), used as a sniping position by the British 95th Foot (Rifles) throughout much of the battle. Beyond, on the other side of the road, is the **Ferme de la Haie Sainte** (see pages 37–8). Up the hill on this side of the road is the **Hanoverian Monument** (see page 43), a large stone obelisk erected in 1818. On the opposite side of the road is the **Gordon Monument** (see page 42), a fluted column, to Wellington's aide-de-camp who was wounded by a roundshot to the hip

The French cuirassiers were heavy cavalry distinguished by their cuirass breastplate armour (© WBT/Alex Kouprianoff)

The Marcognet Monument stands close to the midpoint of the ridge to the east of Wellington's crossroads (© Antony Mason)

when rallying British and Brunswicker troops when under pressure from the Middle Guard towards the end of the battle; he breathed his last in Wellington's bed at his Waterloo HQ. This memorial was erected in 1817. Note how both the Gordon Memorial and the Hanoverian Memorial stand on knolls well above the surrounding land. This is because they once stood on the high banks that lined the road, but earth from all around here was excavated to build the Butte du Lion.

Go back to the crossroads. At the northeast corner is the **Belgian Monument** (see page 43), erected and inaugurated in haste in 1914, as a new war loomed. Cross the busy N5 (with care) at the pedestrian crossing. This is **Wellington's crossroads**, at the centre of his line. An elm tree at the southwestern angle provided a focal point from which he could conduct the battle. He moved constantly up and down his lines, but returned here frequently. The elm tree survived the battle but was cut down by the landowner in 1818 to stop the many tourists trampling his crops, and the wood was made into souvenirs and furniture. Looking from here, you can see the critical danger posed by the capture by the French of the Ferme de la Haie Sainte, just below, at around 18.30.

Continue along the Route du Lion to return to the Hameau du Lion.

A BATTLEFIELD TOUR BY CAR

Having a car makes it possible to visit all the main sites of the battlefield easily and efficiently. Essentially the battlefield is on a north–south axis created by the Brussels–Charleroi road (the N5), as indeed it was in 1815. This journey covers only about 20km in all, there and back, but you will need a full day (or at least five–six hours) to see everything, see map, page 32.

WELLINGTON'S GROUND Start at the centre of Waterloo Town (there is parking behind the Tourist Office), and visit the **Musée Wellington** (see page 41). After this, go back across the road to see the **Chapelle Royale and Eglise Saint-Joseph** (see page 41).

Now head south along the busy N5, through Waterloo Town. After 2.5km you come to a big roundabout where the road to Nivelles (Chaussée de Nivelles, N27) leads off to the right. Continue straight on, on the N5. On the left you will see the **Ferme de Mont-Saint-Jean** (see pages 35–6), the Anglo-Allied medical station during the battle. A little further on you come to traffic lights at a crossroads. Turn right to visit the **Hameau du Lion**, the battlefield centre beside the giant mound with the lion on top (the Butte du Lion). Park here to visit the new **visitor centre** and **Panorama**, and to climb the **Butte du Lion** (see pages 31–4).

Now either walk back to the crossroads on the N5, or drive back, if you can park nearby. This is **Wellington's crossroads**, which stood at the centre of his line; an elm tree at the southwestern angle was effectively his battlefield headquarters. The Anglo-Allied lines stretched for about 1.5km east and west of here, along the ridge. The fluted column on the slope beyond where the elm tree stood is the **Gordon Monument** (see page 42). Use the pedestrian crossing at the lights to cross the N5 (take care). On the other side you will see the **Belgian Monument** (see page 43) at the northeastern angle of the crossroads, and beyond that two steles (stones with brass plaques on either side of the road): the **Inniskilling Monument** (see pages 43–4) and the **Picton Monument** (see page 44).

NAPOLEON'S GROUND   Take the path to the right. This leads down through the trees to the **Ferme de la Haie Sainte** (see pages 37–8), seen across the road. Up the hill on this side of the road is the **Hanoverian Monument** (see page 43), a large stone obelisk.

Rejoin your car and drive back to the crossroads, turning right to continue along the N5. You are now crossing the battlefield. As you come up the rise, the first building you come to, on the left (painted white) is **La Belle Alliance** (see page 38), the inn that stood in the middle of the French lines, which lined the ridge to the east and west of this point. You can draw in off the road to the right-hand side. A little walk down the farm track leading west will give you a chance to look back across the valley to the ridge where Wellington's army lined up. Continue down the N5 for just some 200m (past La Saline restaurant; see page 71). First you will see the **Victor**

French cuirassiers charge the Anglo-Allied squares, as depicted in Louis Dumoulin's painting in the Panorama
(© Louis Dumoulin)

Hugo Monument (the tall pillar on the left; see page 44–5), and then the **Wounded Eagle Monument** (see page 44) on the right-hand side. Again you can draw in on the right-hand side to see these monuments more closely – worth doing certainly for the Wounded Eagle Monument. Do be careful if you try to cross the road.

Continue south on the N5 for 2.5km to reach the **Ferme du Caillou**, Napoleon's last headquarters (see page 36), an old farm set beside the road, which contains an interesting little museum, centring on Napoleon. Now head north again, back towards the battlefield, but take the first right to go to **Plancenoit**. When you reach the village, find the Place de Plancenoit to reach the village green at the centre, overlooked by the church (and Le Gros Vélo restaurant; see page 71). This was the scene of desperate hand-to-hand fighting towards the end of the Battle of Waterloo, as the Prussians under General Bülow fought to dislodge the French under Lieutenant General Lobau, reinforced by the Young Guard under Lieutenant General Duhesme. Plancenoit changed hands several times before the Prussians prevailed. The church – although largely rebuilt after the battle – still resembles how it looked at the time, and bears some memorial plaques to the French. Continue around the village green, following signs to the Monument aux Prussiens. The **Prussian Monument** (see page 45) stands where their artillery was sited as they attempted to take Plancenoit. You can now continue west to return to La Belle Alliance.

From here you can turn right to return to Waterloo Town. If you want to visit the Ferme de Hougoumont, turn left, then first right, after the Wounded Eagle Monument. After about 2km the road crosses the R0 motorway; continue a little further to the crossroads on the old Waterloo–Nivelles road (N27) and turn right here. After about 200m a signpost to the right points to Goumont (may change after 2015). This leads to the **Ferme de Hougoumont** (see pages 34–5), the site of some of the most dramatic and critical fighting during the battle, recently restored.

Go back to the N27 and turn right to return to the centre of Waterloo.

LA ROUTE NAPOLEON EN WALLONIE

When Napoleon brought his Armée du Nord across the border from France on 15 June 1815, he did so in three columns: the Colonne de Gauche (Left Column) with the I Corps and II Corps led by D'Erlon and Reille; the Colonne de Droite (Right Column), with Grouchy's cavalry and the IV Corps led by Gérard; and the Central Column, the 'Marche de l'Empereur' (the Emperor's March), with the III Corps led by Vandamme and the VI Corps led by Lobau. You can follow these routes by car, starting in the south and heading north to Waterloo. The Tourist Offices of Wallonia have marked Napoleon's route with small brown signs (*www. laroutenapoleonenwallonie.be*). They start at Beaumont and essentially head north along the N53 to Charleroi, diverting a little to the east to visit Ham-sur-Heure. Our route largely follows that plan but also diverts along the way to visit places on the route of the Colonne de Gauche. It covers some 90km in all and will take a full day. (Note that the opening times of the various attractions along the way are not generous enough to allow you to see everything in a day, so you will have to be selective.) Many of the recommended sights have a Napoleonic connection, but some are not Napoleonic at all. Warning: signposting on these roads is notoriously inconsistent; a good map will help.

CROSSING THE (OLD) FRONTIER This route starts at Beaumont (70km south of Waterloo). In 1815, the border lay to the north here, so this was still in France. Beaumont is famous for its Tour Salamandre (*Grand-Place, 6500 Beaumont;* ☎ *071 58 81 91; http://beaumont.be;* ⊕ *May–Jun & Sep 10.00–16.30 Thu–Tue, Jul–Aug 10.00–17.30 Thu–Tue; Oct 10.00–16.30 Sun only; adult/child €3/€2*), the last remnant of the town's medieval fortifications, dating from the 11th century; it now contains a museum of local history and crafts. More to the point, it has views over the place where Napoleon's army first bivouacked on 14 June. Napoleon himself stayed the nights of 14 and 15 June on the Place de Beaumont, at the Château de Beaumont des Princes de Caraman (now a school), owned by the Prince of Chimay, freshly elevated to Baron of the Empire; it has a commemorative plaque bearing the imperial eagle.

The terraced 'hanging gardens' of Thuin are linked to its history as a fortified town (© WBT/JL Flémal)

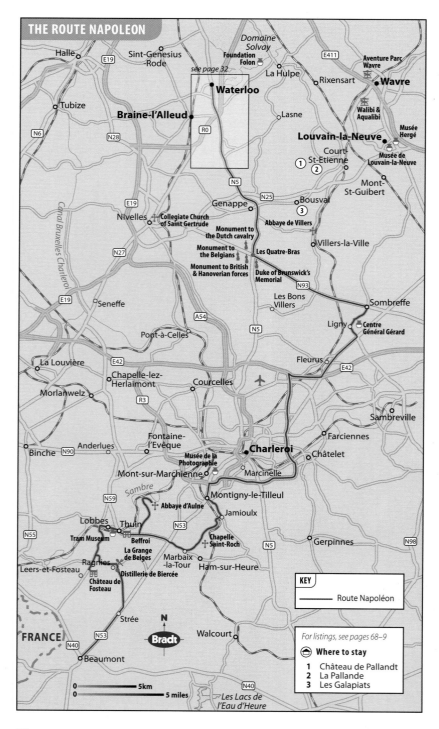

THE ROUTE NAPOLEON

Halle
Sint-Genesius-Rode
E19
Tubize
Braine-l'Alleud
N6
N28
R0

Domaine Solvay
Foundation Folon
see page 32
Waterloo

E411
Aventure Parc Wavre
La Hulpe
Rixensart
Wavre
Walibi & Aqualibi
Lasne
Louvain-la-Neuve
Musée Hergé
Court-St-Etienne
Musée de Louvain-la-Neuve
Mont-St-Guibert
1
2

N5
E19
Nivelles
Collegiate Church of Saint Gertrude
Genappe
N25
Bousval
3
Abbaye de Villers
Monument to the Dutch cavalry
Monument to the Belgians
Les Quatre-Bras
Villers-la-Ville
Monument to British & Hanoverian forces
Duke of Brunswick's Memorial
N27
N93
Les Bons Villers
Sombreffe
Seneffe
A54
Ligny
Centre Général Gérard
Pont-à-Celles
N5
E19
La Louvière
E42
Fleurus
E42
Chapelle-lez-Herlaimont
Courcelles
Morlanwelz
R3
Sambreville
Fontaine-l'Evêque
Farciennes
Anderlues
Charleroi
Binche
N90
Musée de la Photographie
Châtelet
Mont-sur-Marchienne
Marcinelle
Sambre
Montigny-le-Tilleul
N59
Abbaye d'Aulne
Jamioulx
Lobbes
Thuin
N53
Tram Museum
Beffroi
Chapelle Saint-Roch
N5
Gerpinnes
N98
N55
La Grange de Belges
Marbaix-la-Tour
Ragnies
Distillerie de Biercée
Ham-sur-Heure
Leers-et-Fosteau
Château de Fosteau
Strée
N
FRANCE
N53
Walcourt
Bradt
N40
Beaumont

KEY
——— Route Napoléon

For listings, see pages 68–9
Where to stay
1 Château de Pallandt
2 La Pallande
3 Les Galapiats

0 ————— 5km
0 ————— 5 miles
N40
Les Lacs de l'Eau d'Heure

Antique distillery equipment in the courtyard of the Distillerie de Biercée (© Antony Mason)

Continue north on the N53, following the Route Napoléon. At Strée you have the option to leave that route for a while to visit a distillery and a castle.

Take a left-hand turn at Strée to follow the road to Ragnies, where you will find a beautiful old fortified farmhouse, the Ferme de la Cour, once the medieval courts of justice of the Abbey of Lobbes, and now home to the Distillerie de Biercée (*36 Rue de la Roquette, 6532 Ragnies;* ✆ *071 50 00 50; www.distilleriedebiercee.be;* ⊕ *Apr–Sep noon–18.00 Tue–Sun, late Mar & Oct–mid-Nov noon–18.00 Sat–Sun only*). It is worth dropping in just to visit this building, see a small exhibition of historic distilling equipment, visit the shop, or eat in the brasserie La Grange de Belges. But you can also take a guided tour of the distillery (⊕ *Apr–Sep 15.00 Tue–Sun, late Mar & Oct–mid-Nov 15.00 Sat–Sun only; adult/child 6–18 €7/€3.50 (inc tasting for adults)*). The distillery is famous for its fruit-based alcohols, notably the lemon-based L'Eau de Villée. It also distils the fruit ingredients for Mandarine Napoléon, a drink originally made from mandarins for Napoleon by his physician Antoine-François de Fourcroy in about 1806. It was produced only on a commercial scale after 1892, and the company was later taken over by Fourcroy's descendants; it is now owned by the Dutch distillers De Kuyper.

ROUTE OF THE COLONNE DE GAUCHE The N561 leads west: continue along this to reach the crossroads with the N559, and turn south to Leers-et-Fosteau. Here you will find the **Château de Fosteau** (*1 Rue du Marquis, 6530 Leers-et-Fosteau;* ✆ *071 59 23 44; www.chateaufosteau.be;* ⊕ *Apr–mid-Dec 14.00–18.00 Thu–Mon, mid-Dec–Mar 14.00–18.00 Sat–Sun only; adult/child 12–18 & student & senior €3/€2.50; guided tours by request*). This fine stone-and-brick château, dating from the 14th century, has a Gothic 'Knight's Hall', a little pharmacy museum, and a bedroom recording the visit of Lieutenant General Honoré Charles Reille, commander of Napoleon's II Corps, who stayed on the night of 15 June 1815.

You can continue up the N559 on the route of the Colonne de Gauche to the hilltop town of **Thuin**, where Napoleon's army skirmished with the Prussians on the morning of 15 June 1815. Thuin has a UNESCO-listed **Beffroi** (*Belfry; Pl du Chapitre, 6530 Thuin;* ✆ *071 55 49 18; www.hainauttourisme.be/unesco/beffroi-de-thuin;* ⊕ *Apr–Sep 10.00–noon & 13.00–18.00 Tue–Sun, Jul–Aug 10.00–noon & 13.00–18.00 daily, Oct 10.00–noon & 13.00–17.00 Tue–Sun; adult/child/under 12 €3/€1/free*), dating

from 1639, with fine views from the top of its 194 steps. There is also a charming little **tram museum** at Thuin, the Centre de Découverte du Chemin de Fer Vicinal (*2a Rue du Fosteau, 6530 Thuin;* ☏ *071 37 00 05; www.asvi.be;* ☉ *Apr–Oct 11.00–16.00 Thu, 11.00–18.00 Sat–Sun; museum only adult/child under 12 €3/free; museum + rides adult/child under 12 €9/free*). Run by enthusiasts of the ASVi (Association pour la Sauvegarde du Vicinal – Association for the Preservation of the Local Railway), it presents about 30 beautifully restored historic trams, and runs a regular schedule of tram rides in historic trams on Saturdays and Sundays and other 'special days'.

After Thuin, head back towards the N53 by taking the N59. A road to the left leads eventually, after about 5km, to the extensive ruins of the **Abbaye d'Aulne** (*275 Rue Emile Vandervelde, 6534 Thuin;* ☏ *071 59 54 54; www.abbayedaulne.be;* ☉ *Apr–Jun & Sep 13.00–18.00 Wed–Sun, Jul–Aug 13.00–18.00 daily, Oct 13.00–17.00 Wed–Sun; adult/seniors & child 12–18/child under 12 €4/€3/free*). Said to have been founded in AD657 by St Landelin, it became a prosperous Cistercian monastery before destruction by the French Revolutionary Army in 1794. A brewery, the Brasserie du Val de Sambre, has been set up in the old 18th-century stables, producing a beer named Abbaye d'Aulne, and has a tavern serving the beer and light meals (☉ *summer 13.00–20.00 daily, winter Sat–Sun*).

IN NAPOLEON'S FOOTSTEPS Now return to the N53 to rejoin the Route Napoléon. At Gozée, go straight over the crossroads towards Ham-sur-Heure. Driving through pretty countryside beside the river Eau d'Heure, the Route Napoléon signs take you to the **Chapelle Saint-Roch**. (*31 Chemin des Trois Arbres, 6120 Ham-sur-Heure*). This tiny stone chapel – more like a kiosk with a spire – is the focus of processions in honour of St Roch, in the tradition of the 'Marches de l'Entre Sambre-et Meuse', essentially religious processions, but in which participants dress in historic, often Napoleonic-style uniforms (see pages 6–7).

The Route Napoléon now winds its way towards Charleroi, where it rejoins the N53. This is

Thuin's belfry, a UNESCO World Heritage site (© OPT/JL Flémal)

an opportunity to visit the excellent **Musée de la Photographie** (*11 Av Paul Pastur, 6032 Charleroi; ☏ 071 43 58 10; www.museephoto.be; ⏲ 10.00– 18.00 Tue–Sun; adult/senior/student/ child under 12 €6/€4/€3/free*), which lies beside the N53 just to the north of the R3 ring road in the southern suburb of Charleroi called Mont-sur-Marchienne. Housed in a converted neogothic Carmelite convent, as well as a new purpose-built wing, this museum has a comprehensive range of classic photos among its permanent collection of 80,000, 800 or so of which are shown at any one time. The museum also puts on powerful temporary exhibitions. The café overlooks a large park.

Historic trams at Thuin's tram museum (© AVSi)

NAPOLEON'S LAST VICTORY The Route Napoléon now continues through Charleroi to join the N29 to Fleurus. Charleroi was utterly transformed as an industrial centre after Napoleon's day, so you would be justified in scooting around it by going back south a short way and taking the R3 ring road, then turning onto the E42 motorway and coming off at the Fleurus exit to join the N29. Napoleon stayed the night of 16 June at the Château de la Paix (now the town hall) at Fleurus, after the Battle of Ligny. Continue on the N29 for 4km, then turn left to Ligny. This is the site of Napoleon's last victory, against the Prussians, on 16 June 1815. A museum in an old farmhouse in the village commemorates the battle: this the **Centre Général Gérard** (*23 Rue Pont-Piraux, 5140 Ligny; ☏ 071 81 83 13; ⏲ 13.00–17.00 Thu–Mon; adult €4*). On two floors, it tells the story of the Battle of Ligny through maps and models, and has a few uniforms, muskets and cannonballs, badges, buttons and surgical instruments. The labelling is in French. Lieutenant General Maurice Gérard was a French hero of the Battle of Ligny. On 18 June, it was he who tried to persuade Grouchy, heading to Wavre, to change course to 'follow the sound of the cannons' coming from Waterloo, but Grouchy would not be diverted: if he had done so, the result of the Battle of Waterloo might have been very different.

4

QUATRE-BRAS Continue north out of Ligny to join the N93 (the Namur–Nivelles road) and along the Route Napoléon to **Les Quatre-Bras** – the crossroads with the N5 (Charleroi–Brussels road). This is the site of the other battle of 16 June 1815, between the French (under Marshal Ney) and Anglo-Allied forces (under Wellington), which ended inconclusively and with the ordered retreat of the Anglo-Allied forces to Waterloo. Today it is just an ordinary crossroads flanked by a few commercial enterprises, but there are several monuments here. The most impressive is the **Duke of Brunswick's Memorial**, erected in 1890 on the eastern side of

A signpost on the Route Napoléon (© Antony Mason)

The Château de la Hulpe in the Domaine Solvay (© Emilianm/Dreamstime.com)

the road, 400m south in the direction of Charleroi. A bronze Dutch–Belgian lion stands on a high plinth, its paw resting on a shield bearing the Brunswick coat of arms. He was mortally wounded by a musket ball to his wrist and stomach and died after being carried to a nearby farmhouse. On the Nivelles road, 150m to the west of the crossroads, is a modern stone **monument to British and Hanoverian forces** that fought at Quatre-Bras, with a list of their divisions, brigades and regiments; it was inaugurated by the 8th Duke of Wellington in 2002. A little further west, on the north side of the road, is a curious sword-like monument erected in 1990 to honour the **Dutch cavalry** regiments. A further 200m, on the left-hand side, is a stone **monument to the Belgians** who were killed at Quatre-Bras, erected in 1926. It says, in French, that they died 'for the defence of the flag and the honour of arms', carefully avoiding any mention of which side they fought on.

The road north from Quatre-Bras, the N5, leads to Waterloo, passing the **Ferme du Caillou** (see page 36) – Napoleon's last headquarters before the Battle of Waterloo – and then crosses the battlefield itself.

EXCURSIONS AROUND WATERLOO Map, page 56.

FONDATION FOLON AND THE DOMAINE SOLVAY (*4km northeast of Waterloo Town*) The Domaine Solvay is a beautiful 560ha public park, with woodland and lakes on the edge of the Forêt de Soignes. At its heart is the 19th-century Château de la Hulpe, which was bought in 1893 by the wealthy industrialist and philanthropist Ernest Solvay (1838–1922), the inventor of a patented process to make industrial soda (used in the manufacture of glass, steel, detergents and dyes). The Solvay family gave the estate to the nation in 1972 and today the château is used only for private receptions and seminars, but its farm complex houses the **Fondation Folon** (*Ferme du Château de la Hulpe, 6a Drève de la Ramée, 1310 La Hulpe;* ☏ *02 653 34 56; www.fondationfolon.be;* ⊕ *Mar–Oct 10.00–18.00 Tue–Sun, Nov–Feb 10.00–17.00 Tue–Sun; adult/student & senior/child 6–12 €9/€7/€5; note that the car park is 400m from the museum*). The Walloon painter, illustrator and sculptor Jean-Michel Folon (1934–2004), known simply as Folon, had a charming and distinctive style which most people will probably recognise even if they did not know his name – for, over his lifetime, his illustrations appeared in countless magazines, posters, stamps, books and much else. His bright watercolour washes and stylised figures are mixed with wry poetic whimsy – and that is the overarching mood of this beguiling museum, which exhibits

'Miami, un soir' by Folon, using his characteristic watercolour wash (© Folon)

more than 500 examples of his illustrations along with sculpture, installations and audiovisual presentations. It is an art museum that will delight all the family.

WAVRE (*15km east of Waterloo*) Capital of the Province of Brabant Wallon, Wavre is a busy and attractive town. There is little now to recall that this was the scene of ferocious fighting in the late afternoon of 18 June 1815, when the French under Marshal Grouchy set about winkling out Prussian forces defending buildings lining the river Dyle at Wavre, Bierges and Limal. In the end he prevailed late in the evening, but it was a useless victory: Prussian forces under Blücher, Bülow and Ziethen had slipped away earlier in the day and tipped the balance at Waterloo into an Allied victory, and Grouchy had to retreat with the other surviving French forces.

A famous statue (1962) in the town centre, by the town hall, depicts a mischievous boy of folklore climbing a wall: this is 'Maca', with whom the people of Wavre happily identify themselves, and will stroke his bare buttocks to bring them luck for a year. Wavre is also famous for the large theme park on its outskirts, called **Walibi** (*1300 Limal;* ☏ *010 42 15 00; www.walibi.be;* ⊕ *Easter holidays & w/ends in Apr, mid-Jun–mid-Jul, Sep–Oct & All Saints' holiday 10.00–18.00, mid-Jul–Aug 10.00–20.00, but check online for schedules; adult/senior & child 1–1.4m/child under 1m €36/€31/free*). The name is not just an Australian marsupial (its mascot) but a combination of the three surrounding communities: Wavre, Limal and Bierges. Set around lakes in a spacious park, Walibi offers a host of rides and attractions from

One of the pedestrian-friendly streets in the centre of Wavre (© WBT/JP Remy)

WAVRE CHEESECAKE

Wavre is famous for its *Tarte au Stofé de Wavre*, a cheesecake made – like most *tartes au fromage* – with *fromage blanc* (a kind of cream cheese), beaten egg and sugar. The difference is that it also contains ground almonds and crushed almond-macaroon biscuits, plus a layer of stewed apples – ideally mildly acidic *pommes reinettes* (pippin apples). *Stofé* is the Walloon word for *fromage blanc*. The recipe is said to date from the 13th century.

the very gentle (for the youngest visitors) to the most heart-stopping: the Loup-Garou (werewolf) rollercoaster over 1km long, Vampire Terror, the Challenge of Tutankhamen, Calamity Mine train, Radja River ride, and so on. The park also has plenty of restaurants and food outlets, to cater for a full day out. It also includes a separate swimming complex called **Aqualibi** (*100 Bd de l'Europe, 1300 Wavre;* ☎ *010 42 16 03; www.aqualibi.be; similar schedule to Walibi, plus winter schedule Wed & Fri–Sun; adult/senior & child 1.2–1.4m/child 1–1.2m/child under 1m €19/€15/€5/free*), with jacuzzis, hot baths, a wave pool, tubular shoots and toboggan shoots and rapids. If you plan your day, you can visit both Walibi and Aqualibi.

Some 2km to the northwest of Wavre is **Aventure Parc Wavre** (*152 Sainte-Anne, 1300 Wavre;* ☎ *010 22 33 87; www.aventureparc.be;* ⏰ *mid-Jun–Aug 10.00–18.30 daily, Apr–mid-Jun & Sep–Oct 10.00–18.30 w/ends & public/school holidays; adult & child over 10/child 7–9/child 5–6/child 4 €27–55 depending on the package/€23/€19/€5*). Test your limits with 14 different challenges: rope walks and bridges through the trees, monkey swings, jumps on to a giant mattress, bungee jumping – all under careful supervision and graded according to age.

*The entrance to the Musée Hergé at Louvain-la-Neuve
(© Atelier Christian de Portzamparc 2011)*

Tourist information

**Maison du Tourisme des Ardennes
Brabançonnes**   1 Rue de Nivelles, 1300 Wavre; ☎010 23 03 52; www.mtab.be; ⊕ 08.30–17.00

Mon–Tue, 08.30–17.30 Wed–Sat, 10.00–16.00
Sun

LOUVAIN-LA-NEUVE *(15km southeast of Waterloo)* The purpose-built, innovative and controversial university campus at Louvain-la-Neuve opened in 1980, an uncompromisingly modern complex of departmental facilities and residential blocks, blended with a small, functioning town, all raised on an upper level above the feed roads and railway. It was the outcome of bitter language disputes (Dutch vs French) that in the 1960s tore apart the venerable old Flemish university town of Leuven (Louvain in French), to the east of Brussels. They were resolved by building this new French-language university here at Ottignies in Brabant Wallon, calling it Louvain-la-Neuve (New Leuven). The town itself is interesting to visit from an architectural point of view, but it also has the attraction of two interesting museums. The **Musée Hergé** (*26 Rue du Labrador, 1348 Louvain-la-Neuve;* ☎*010 48 84 21; www.museeherge.com;* ⊕ *10.30–17.30 Tue–Sun; adult/child 7–14* €*9.50/*€*5)*

is *the* Tintin museum, or rather *the* museum dedicated to his creator, Brussels-born Georges Remi (he reversed his initials and wrote how they are pronounced in French: *her-gé*). Set in a stunning modern complex designed by French architect Christian de Portzamparc, it traces Hergé's development and the story of Tintin through many original drawings, prints, mementos, installations and other exhibits. Do not make the mistake of thinking that this is a museum for children: children may enjoy it, but it is really a museum for Tintin enthusiasts.

The **Musée de Louvain-la-Neuve** (*1 Pl Blaise Pascal, 1348 Louvain-la-Neuve; 010 47 48 41; www.museelln.be;* ⏰ *10.00–18.00 Tue–Fri, 14.00–18.00 Sat–Sun; adult/ senior & student/under 18s €3/€2/free*) is the excellent little university museum. It has a small but choice art collection, including plenty of work by big names such as Breughel, Dürer, Goya, Ensor, Picasso, Magritte and Delvaux. It also has a fascinating collection of art and anthropological artefacts from around the world.

Tourist information

Tourism Office-Inforville Galerie des Halles, 1 Pl de l'Université, 1348 Louvain-la-Neuve; 010 47 47 47; www.tourisme-olln.be; ⏰ 09.00–17.00 Mon–Fri, 11.00–17.00 Sat, also Jul–Aug 11.00–17.00 Sun. Located in the pedestrianised centre of Louvain-la-Neuve.

ABBAYE DE VILLERS (*20km southeast of Waterloo; 55 Rue de l'Abbaye, 1495 Villers-la-Ville; 071 88 09 80; www.villers.be;* ⏰ *Apr–Oct 09.00–18.00 Mon & Wed–Fri, 10.00–18.00 Sat–Sun, Nov–Mar 09.00–17.00 Mon & Wed–Fri, 10.00–17.00 Sat–Sun; adult/senior & student/child 6–12 €6/€5/€2.50*) This fine old ruined abbey was founded by Cistercians from Clairvaux in 1146. It developed into a large, powerful institution, with a soaring Gothic abbey church and, in the 18th century, a palatial Neoclassical residence for the abbot. However, it was sacked by the French Revolutionary Army in 1794, and abandoned two years later. What remains is a vast and atmospheric ruin of stone and brick, bearing witness to six centuries of

The ruins of the church, cloister, refectory and other monastic buildings at the Abbaye de Villers (© WBT/JL Flémal)

The nave of the Collegiate Church of St Gertrude, Nivelles (© Antony Mason)

activity brought to a sudden end just 200 years ago. Tucked in the base of a wooded valley, it also has an air of profound tranquillity. The choir of the great abbey church is still covered by a high vault, giving it haunting acoustics that are demonstrated occasionally by singers leading tours, and by a programme of summer concerts. Elsewhere, there are the remains of stables, workshops, a brewery, pilgrims' lodgings, refectories – even a dank little prison for miscreants awaiting trial in the church courts. Renovations are under way to develop the old abbey mill outside the main enclosure to become the new entrance, with a shop, tavern, restaurant and exhibition spaces, due to open in summer 2015.

Tourist information

Maison du Tourisme du Pays de Villers en Brabant Wallon 55 Rue de l'Abbaye, 1495 Villers-la-Ville;☎071 88 09 80; www.paysdevillers-tourisme.be; ⊕ Apr–Oct

09.00–18.00 Mon & Wed–Fri, 10.00–18.00 Sat–Sun, Nov–Mar 09.00–17.00 Mon & Wed–Fri, 10.00–17.00 Sat–Sun

4

NIVELLES The pretty little town of Nivelles is famous above all for its extraordinary central church with is towering, fortress-like west front, the **Collegiate Church of Saint Gertrude** (*Grand-Place, 1400 Nivelles;*☎*067 84 08 64;* ⊕ *09.00–17.00 Mon–Sat, 14.00–17.00 Sun; free; guided tours 14.00 daily, also at 15.30 Sat–Sun; adult/senior & student/child 6–12 €6/€5/€2*). This Westbau, as it is called, is in a Byzantine-influenced style called Ottonian (after the 10th-century Holy Roman Emperors called Otto) and dates from the 11th century. But the church is much older still, and goes right back to the time of Saint Gertrude (c621–59), a noblewoman of the Frankish Merovingian dynasty, who founded a chapel on this site. A pilgrimage cult grew up around the relics of St Gertrude, to which miracles were ascribed. Later a Chapter, or College, of Canonesses of St Gertrude emerged, and this was their Collegiate Church. Churches on the site were subsequently destroyed 19 times, the last by German bombing in 1940 (which also destroyed much of the historic centre of Nivelles). This explains the rough, pared-down surfaces of the restored columns and walls inside the church; but the essential form of the 11th-century, 100m-long

Romanesque nave has survived. In the choir the ornate 16th-century housing for the reliquary of St Gertrude can be seen on a raised plinth, but the original 13th-century reliquary – a masterpiece of medieval Gothic metalwork – was wrecked in 1940. The remains of St Gertrude are now in a new and controversial silver reliquary (completed 1982) displayed in the chapel to the right of the choir. It is this reliquary that is taken each year on its 15th-century horse-drawn carriage (on show at the base of the nave) in the procession called the Tour Sainte-Gertrude, which follows a route around Nivelles and the surrounding countryside on the Sunday after Michaelmas (end September/early October). Guided tours of the church take visitors to otherwise inaccessible parts, including the archaeological remains under the nave (where St Gertrude's tomb and royal graves can be seen), the 11th-century crypt, the 13th-century cloister, and high up into the Westbau to the 'Imperial Hall' where a replica of the 13th-century reliquary can be seen, as well as fragments of the astonishing original. Although rarely in English, these guided tours are highly recommended: they offer a privileged view of this exceptional church. There is a 49-bell carillon in the Westbau, used to play carillon concerts on Sunday afternoons in July and August.

Tourist information

Office du Tourisme de Nivelles 48 Rue des Saintes, 1400 Nivelles; 067 21 54 13; www.tourisme-nivelles.be; ⏲ 09.00–18.00 daily. This is also the home of the Tourist Office for Roman Païs (067 22 04 44; www.tourisme-roman-pais. be), the broader local region, of which Nivelles is the capital, so named for the Latin-based dialect formerly spoken here.

TARTE AL DJOTE

It is said that there are two reasons to visit Nivelles: one to see the Collegiate Church of St Gertrude, and the other to eat the local speciality, *Tarte al Djote*. This is a savoury tart made with local cheese called *Boulette de Nivelles* and chopped Swiss chard *(djote)*. It is made in two varieties: *'verte'* (green) and *'mitoyenne'*, which is half green and half white (ie: half does not have the Swiss chard in it). The Nivellois say it has to be served *'bin tchaude, bin blète è qu'èl bûre dèsglète'* (hot, ripe and dripping with butter), but the pungent cheese and fatty content make it something of an acquired taste. You can try it at a boulangerie and café right beside the church: the Boulangerie Le Fournil (*35 Grand-Place;* ⏲ *06.45–17.30 Tue–Sun*).

Speciality of Nivelles: Tarte al Djote (© Antony Mason)

Where to Stay and Eat

Waterloo is only 15km south of Brussels, and many visitors come to the battlefield just for the day. There are, of course, numerous hotels in Brussels. Waterloo, however, is a pleasant and convenient place to stay, and the list below (with the exception of the campsites) cites only accommodation in the immediate vicinity. The majority of the hotels are in Waterloo town centre, which is 4km north of the battlefield. The exception is Le 1815, which is actually on the battlefield. Good bed-and-breakfast accommodation is also available in various locations around the battlefield. Prices quoted are for a double room for one night. Note that – as in Brussels – weekend rates can be much cheaper (often half-price) in Waterloo, because the hotels are primarily geared to weekday business travellers.

HOTELS
Waterloo Town

🏠 **Le Côté Vert** (47 rooms) 200G Chaussée de Bruxelles, 1410 Waterloo; ☎ 02 354 01 05; e info@cotevert.be; www.cotevert.be. A restful, modern hotel set in lantern-lit gardens away from the busy Chaussée de Bruxelles, & a short walk from the Musée Wellington, tourist office & high-street shops. Has its own, respected restaurant (La Cuisine au Vert). Fitness suite. Free parking. Free Wi-Fi throughout. B/fast is included in the price. Also has 2-bedroom studio apartments. €165

The garden at Le Côté Vert hotel, Waterloo (© Hôtel Le Côté Vert)

Waterloo has its own beer called 'Waterloo'. It is brewed at Braine-l'Alleud by the Brasserie de Waterloo, a branch of the Martin's Group (which owns a large number of other brands, including Dominus, Timmermans and Bourgogne des Flandres; *www.anthonymartin.be*). 'Waterloo' comes in two forms: Strong Dark (8.5% ABV); and Triple Blond (7.5%). Other breweries in Walloon Brabant include the Brasserie Lefebvre at Quenast (*20km west of Waterloo; www.brasserielefebvre.be*), which has been brewing since 1876 and produces a large range of brands, in various manifestations, including the 'abbey beer' Floreffe, fruit beers such as Belgian Kriek, Hopus and Barbãr. From its farm brewery at Baisy-Thy, near Les Quatre-Bras, the Brasserie du Brabant (*15km south of Waterloo; www.labrasseriedubrabant.net*) produces the artisan-beer in its La Brabançonne range: La Brabançonne Ambrée (7.5% ABV); Brune (9.1%); Blonde au Miel (with honey; 6.5%); and the Christmas beer La Moche de Noël (9%).

Wine is made in a number of places in Brabant Wallon. The best known is the Domaine de Mellemont (*www.domaine-de-mellemont.com*), established in 1993 at Thorembais-les-Béguines, east of Louvain-la-Neuve. It makes white, red and rosé wines, and sparkling wines called 'Bulles pour Elle' and 'Bulles pour Lui'.

Martin's Grand Hotel Waterloo (79 rooms) 198 Chaussée de Tervuren, 1410 Waterloo; 02 352 18 15; e mgh@martinshotels.com; www.martinshotels.com. An elegant, luxurious & polished 4-star hotel in the upmarket Martin's chain, set in the surprisingly grand buildings of a former sugar factory, built in 1836 (best observed in the Roman-bath-like architecture of its high-quality restaurant, La Sucrerie). Quiet location, about 1km from Waterloo town centre. Fitness/health club. Free parking. Free Wi-Fi throughout. B/fast is included in the price. €180

Martin's Lodge (29 rooms) 198 Chaussée de Tervuren, 1410 Waterloo; 02 352 18 15; e mlo@martinshotels.com; www.martinshotels.com. The 3-star little sister of the Martin's Grand, right next door, offering modern comfort without the luxury extras. Fitness/health club. Free parking. Free Wi-Fi throughout. B/fast is inc. €100

Ibis Brussels Waterloo (72 rooms) 5 Bd Henri Rolin, 1410 Waterloo; 02 351 0030; e ibiswaterloo@cgmhotels.com; www.ibis.com. Standard, good-quality Ibis fare, presentable & businesslike, close to the heart of Waterloo. Free parking. Free Wi-Fi throughout. B/fast is not included in the price. €95

Waterloo battlefield

Le 1815 Hotel (15 rooms) 367 Route du Lion, 1410 Waterloo; 02 387 01 60; e indo@

le1815.be; www.le1815.be. This relaxed & agreeable little hotel has the key advantage of being on the battlefield, close to the crossroads from where Wellington directed the battle & 400m from the Butte du Lion. Recently renovated, all the rooms are named after leading generals in the battle. One disadvantage is that it is 4km from the centre of Waterloo Town, so a little isolated, but it has its own (good) restaurant, & there are 2 other restaurants (the pizzeria Les Deux Sil & the bistro L'Estaminet de Joséphine) close by. Free parking. Wi-Fi at €5 per 24hrs. B/fast is not included in the price. €100

BED AND BREAKFAST
Lasne/Plancenoit

Le Vert Logis (2 rooms) 517 Chaussée de Louvain, 1380 Ohain (Lasne); 02 354 78 02; e bertrandmignot@skynet.be; www.levertlogis.be. Very stylish B&B overlooking a garden & tranquil rural views, 3km east of the centre of Waterloo, 5km from the battlefield. Free Wi-Fi. €75

Nicoline (1 room) 7 Av Maréchal Ney, 1380 Plancenoit; 02 633 31 51; e degrox.michel@belgacom.net; www.chambre-hotes-plancenoit.be. Beautifully presented B&B close to the centre of the pretty village of Plancenoit. Free Wi-Fi. €70

Bousval/Genappe

Château de Pallandt (4 rooms) 15 Rue Bois des Conins, 1470 Bousval-Genappe; 010

61 39 63; **e** ehooghvoorst@skynet.be; www.
chateau-de-pallandt.be. A château that has been
in the same family for 3 centuries (remodelled in
the early 20th), surrounded by 100ha of woodland,
provides a spectacularly grand setting for a B&B,
17km southeast of Waterloo. Free Wi-Fi. Heated
swimming pool (seasonal); tennis. €115

La Pallande (5 rooms) 66 Chemin de Wavre,
1470 Genappe; **✆**0472 20 50 66; www.lapallande.
be. A large 19th-century house overlooking lakes,
with attractively decorated rooms. Free Wi-Fi.
16km southeast of Waterloo. €70

Les Galapiats (2 rooms) 30 Rue du
Château, 1470 Bousval; **✆**067 77 30 60; **e** info@
lesgalapiats.be; www.lesgalapiats.be. Tidy modern
rooms in a late 19th-century home in a rural
setting, with a pottery studio attached, 15km
southeast of Waterloo. €70

CAMPSITES

Ⅹ Camping Au Val Tourinnes 48 Rue du
Grand Brou, 1320 Tourinnes-la-Grosse; **✆**010 86
66 42; **e** info@campingauvaltourinnes.com; www.
campingauvaltourinnes.com. Situated 42km to
the east of Waterloo (closer to Wavre & Louvain-
la-Neuve) this is a 3-star site with 75 pitches
(tents, caravans, motorhomes) with lakes & sports
activities.

Ⅹ Bruxelles Europe à Ciel Ouvert 205
Chaussée de Wavre, 1050 Brussels; **✆**02 270
95 97; **e** cielouvertcamping@yahoo.fr; www.
cielouvertcamping.wordpress.com. Tents only
(50 pitches), & just for the months of Jul & Aug,
but this offers camping close to the European
Parliament & the centre of Brussels, in the suburb
of Ixelles.

✖ WHERE TO EAT AND DRINK *Map, pages 8 and 32.*

Prices quoted are the typical cost of a main course.

WATERLOO TOWN

✖ L'Amusoir 121 Chaussée de Bruxelles,
1410 Waterloo; **✆**02 354 82 33; www.lamusoir.
be; ⏰ noon–14.30 & 19.00–22.30 Sun–Wed,
noon–14.30 & 19.00–midnight Thu–Sat. From the
outside it looks modest, but inside is a large (yet
intimate) tavern-like restaurant with a beamed
roof & log-cabin décor offset by movie-star photos.

It has a real buzz of popularity matched by a busy
team of staff rushing dishes out from an open
kitchen. From a pre-printed menu, choose grilled
steaks, fish dishes, Belgian classics, meal-sized
salads, burgers, pasta. Large garden with pond in
summer. Also has a separate, cosy bar within the
restaurant. €16

♉ Oscar's 200 Chaussée de Bruxelles, 1410
Waterloo; **✆**02 354 79 27; ⏰ 11.00–02.00 Mon–
Thu, 11.00–03.30 Fri–Sat. Large modern bar with

WATERLOO'S SUGAR TART

Waterloo was a sugar town: its *sucrerie* (now the Martin's Grand Hotel) first opened in 1837, using the local sugar beet. Waterloo households used its product to make a *tarte au sucre brun* – essentially soft brown sugar piled onto a short-crust pastry mould, dotted with clumps of butter and covered with a scant layer of beaten egg mixed with fresh cream, then baked until soft, speckled and caramelised. The *tarte* is sometimes called *la tarte du Paveû*: *paveurs* (specialist workers from Waterloo who laid cobbled roads) used to receive a gift of brown sugar on saints' feast days. The integrity of Waterloo sugar tart is protected by the Confrérie des Maîtres Paveûs, Scribeux et Mougneux de la Tarte au Sucre (Brotherhood of the Master Pavers, Writers and Eaters of Sugar Tarts), founded in 1993.

night-clubby décor, with a good range of Belgian beers; young crowd, welcoming atmosphere. Has a separate smoking section.

✕ Momo la Crevette 202 Chaussée de Bruxelles, 1410 Waterloo; ☎ 02 352 21 00; www.momolacrevette.mobi; ⏰ noon–14.30 & 19.00–22.30 Tue–Sat. A bright, dynamic fish & seafood restaurant, offering French-style dishes (scallops in champagne, bouillabaisse, skate with caper sauce) as well as the Belgian classics *Tomate aux crevettes & Croquettes aux crevettes*. €25

✕ Le Pain Quotidien 139a Chaussée de Bruxelles, 1410 Waterloo; ☎ 02 354 54 90; www.lepainquotidien.be; ⏰ 07.00–18.30 Mon–Sat, 07.30–17.30 Sun. A Belgian original, founded in Brussels in 1990, & now a well-known international chain, but why not test it in its homeland to see why it is so successful? Coffee & cakes, soup, huge open sandwiches (*tartines*), pasta & other light meals, served in country-kitchen style. Garden at the back in summer. €10

♉ Touchdown 6 Rue de la Station, 1410 Waterloo; ☎ 02 354 03 05; ⏰ 10.00–02.00 Sun–Thu, 10.00–04.00 Fri–Sat. A huge, atmospherically dingy sports bar with 10 screens & snooker & pool tables. Good Belgian beers, plus coffee & tea, but no food.

✕ Ciao Pizza 10 Rue François Libert, 1410 Waterloo; ☎ 02 351 16 51; www.ciao-pizza.be; ⏰ noon–14.30 & 18.30–22.30 Wed–Sun, noon–14.30 Mon. Central Waterloo location (behind the Tourist Office) for pizzas with *mozzarella di bufala*, pasta & a selection of classic Italian dishes. Attractive, antique–modern décor; terraced formal garden in summer. €13

♉ Twins Lounge 151 Chaussée de Bruxelles, 1410 Waterloo; ☎ 023 51 80 66; www.twinsbar.be;

⏰ 17.00–02.00 Tue–Wed, 17.00–04.00 Thu–Sat. A modern, atmospheric & relaxed bar, close to the Musée Wellington, with a good range of beers & wines. Karaoke on Thu.

⬛ La Brioche 161 Chaussée de Bruxelles, 1410 Waterloo; ☎ 02 353 02 22; ⏰ 07.00–18.00 daily. An elegant pâtisserie with tables & chairs at the back for tea, coffee, tarts, cakes & savoury snacks.

✕ EXKi 195 Chaussée de Bruxelles, 1410 Waterloo; ☎ 02 357 32 56; www.exki.be; ⏰ 08.30–18.30 Mon–Sat. The name is how you say exquisite or delicious (*exquis*) in French. Like Le Pain Quotidien, this chain is another Belgian original, founded in Brussels in 2001, & has now gone international. The formula, décor & branding is distinctively clean, bright & cheering, centring on wholesome, health-conscious meals of salads, sandwiches & some hot dishes, all ethically & ecologically sourced, to eat in or take away. €6

✕ La Pepinière 129 Chaussée de Tervuren, 1410 Waterloo; ☎ 02 354 01 74; www.lapepiniere.be; ⏰ noon–14.30 & 19.00–22.30 Sun–Thu, noon–14.30 & 19.00–23.00 Fri–Sat. A huge restaurant with 80 places inside & 120 on the outside terrace – decorated like a grand beach-hut, providing a spacious, relaxed & elegant setting for seafood (lobster, *plateaux de fruits de mer*) as well as Irish & Argentine beef, pasta, vegetarian dishes & much else. €25

♉ The Snug 127 Chaussée de Tervuren, 1410 Waterloo; ☎ 02 354 01 74; www.thesnug.be; ⏰ 11.00–late daily. Cosy, traditional-style Irish pub, with a good range of Belgian beers, plus coffee. There's a pizza-pasta restaurant called Basta next door, as well as La Pepinière (see above) – all under the same ownership.

Housed in the old La Tonnelle Des Delices building, L'Estaminet de Joséphine restaurant overlooks the battlefield close to Wellington's crossroads (© Antony Mason)

WATERLOO BATTLEFIELD

🖵 Wellington Café Route du Lion, 1410 Waterloo; 📞 02 384 67 40; www.restaurantdulion. be; ⏲ 09.00–20.00 daily (kitchen 11.00–17.00), closes midnight Sun. This large & venerable restaurant-café at the foot of the Butte du Lion – serving coffee, cakes, snacks, ice cream, milkshakes, brasserie food & 120 Belgian beers – will move to its new home opposite the Memorial of the Battle of Waterloo visitor centre in 2015.

✕ L'Estaminet de Joséphine 379 Route du Lion, 1410 Waterloo; 📞 02 384 67 40; www. estaminetdejosephine.be; ⏲ noon–14.30 & 19.00–22.30 Wed–Sun. Napoleon's first wife & true love had to get a look-in somewhere. Classic brasserie food in a classic bistro setting (wooden furniture with gingham tablecloths). €15

✕ Les Deux Sil 377 Route du Lion, 1410 Waterloo; 📞 02 384 09 18; www.restolesdeuxsil; ⏲ noon–14.30 & 18.30–22.00 Sun–Fri, 18.30–22.00 Sat. Agreeable pizzeria with a stone oven, also serving a good range of Italian dishes. Outdoor terrace & garden to the rear. €15

✕ La Saline 16 Chaussée de Charleroi, 1380 Plancenoit; 📞 02 384 39 63; www.restolasaline.be; ⏲ noon–14.30 & 19.00–22.00 Wed–Fri, 19.00–22.00 Sat, noon–14.30 Sun & Mon, closed Tue. Seasonal French-style cuisine in an old farmhouse close to La Belle Alliance, with a bright & attractive modern-rustic interior décor. €18

PLANCENOIT

✕ Le Gros Vélo 22 Pl de Plancenoit, 1380 Lasne; 📞 02 633 17 46; ⏲ 11.00–22.00, *bistrot* closed Thu, restaurant closed Wed & Thu. Overlooking the green in the charming little village of Plancenoit, you can forget the vicious fighting that took place here in 1815 to enjoy a typically Belgian, family-run restaurant where the chef cooks (deliciously) what he fancies from the seasonal fare (eg: game dishes in winter), posted in a long list on a blackboard. Drop in for a drink & a light meal at the *bistrot*, or a fuller meal in the restaurant. Modern, unfussy décor. Terrace outside. €20

Appendix 1

GETTING STARTED IN FRENCH

The language of Waterloo and Wallonia is French. Belgian French is very similar to the French spoken in France, except for minor differences: for 70 and 90, for instance, where the French say *soixante-dix* and *quatre-vingt-dix*, the Belgians say *septante* and *nonante*. Most people involved in the tourist industry speak English – and indeed English is fairly widely understood.

Hello/Good day	*Bonjour*	yesterday	*hier*
Good evening	*Bonsoir*	tomorrow	*demain*
Goodbye	*Au revoir*	open	*ouvert*
Good night		closed	*fermé*
(at bedtime)	*Bonne nuit*	railway station	*la gare*
Yes	*Oui*	ticket	*le billet/ticket*
No	*Non*	money	*l'argent*
Thank you	*Merci*	credit card	*une carte de crédit*
Please	*S'il vous plaît*	telephone	*le téléphone*
How are you?	*Comment allez-vous?/Ça va?*	toilet	*les toilettes*
		to eat	*manger*
Very well,		breakfast	*le petit déjeuner*
thank you	*Très bien, merci*	I am vegetarian	*Je suis*
My name is…	*Je m'appelle…*		*végétarien(ne)*
Do you speak		chips/fries	*les frites*
English?	*Parlez-vous anglais?*	beer	*une bière*
I don't understand	*Je ne comprends pas*	wine	*le vin*
Sorry	*Pardon*	water	*l'eau*
Where is…?	*Où est…?*	menu	*la carte*
When?	*Quand?*	set (fixed price)	
How much?	*Combien?*	menu	*un menu*
The bill, please	*L'addition, s'il vous plaît*	1, 2, 3, 4, 5	*un/une, deux, trois, quatre, cinq*
I am ill	*Je suis malade*	6, 7, 8, 9, 10	*six, sept, huit, neuf, dix*
today	*aujourd'hui*		

Appendix 2

FURTHER INFORMATION

BOOKS

Adkin, Mark *The Waterloo Companion: The Complete Guide to History's Most Famous Land Battle* Aurum Press, 2001. The supreme work: it is hard to imagine a more complete account, with every detail meticulously researched, and maps, photographs, illustrations and lists presented in a large A4 format.

Buttery, David *Waterloo Battlefield Guide* Pen and Sword, 2013. A detailed, authoritative guide to the battlefield, combining a blow-by-blow account of the battle with details of what there is to see, with plenty of maps, photographs and paintings.

Clayton, Tim *Waterloo: Four Days that Changed Europe's Destiny* Little, Brown, 2014. A meticulously detailed analysis of events by a specialist in naval and military history, who has also written *Trafalgar*, focusing particularly on the prelude to the battle, and looking from the point of view of all sides, using eyewitness accounts and illustrated with historic paintings and engravings.

Cornwell, Bernard *Waterloo: the History of Four Days, Three Armies and Three Battles* William Collins, 2014. An accessible, readable and well-researched account by a master storyteller, the creator of the Sharpe novels, with plenty of eyewitness accounts and illustrated with maps, historic paintings and engravings.

Corrigan, Gordon *Waterloo: A New History of the Battle and its Armies* Atlantic Books, 2014. A new, vigorous account by a former serving soldier and military historian, and biographer of Wellington, giving a soldier's view of the armies and the battle, illustrated with maps, photographs and historic paintings.

Kershaw, Robert *24 Hours at Waterloo* W H Allen, 2014. This gripping narrative, by a former infantry officer, military historian and battlefield tour guide, gives a blow-by-blow account targeted at the general reader, and brought vividly alive by copious first-hand accounts.

FILM

Waterloo (1970), directed by Sergey Bondarchuk, starring Rod Steiger as Napoleon and Christopher Plummer as Wellington. Worth watching for the battle scenes which involved thousands of extras from the Soviet army: 15,000 infantry, 2,000 cavalry. The sheer weight of numbers is very realistic, and unrepeatable.

Index